DEVELOPING OUR LEADERS FOR THIS CENTURY'S CHALLENGES

Insights from Global Leaders

Edited By Peta Ashworth & Alain de Sales

First published 2021 by Liveris Academy

Liveris Academy acknowledges the Traditional Owners and their custodianship of the lands on which UQP operates. We pay our respects to their Ancestors and their descendants, who continue cultural and spiritual connections to Country. We recognise their valuable contributions to Australian and global society.

Website: https://liveris-academy.uq.edu.au/
Email: liverisacademy@uq.edu.au

Cover design by Catucci Designs
Typeset in 13/17 pt Adobe Garamond Pro by Post Pre-press Group, Brisbane
Printed in Australia by UQ Print

A catalogue record for this book is available from the National Library of Australia.

ISBN 978 0 6453 4090 7 (pbk)
ISBN 978 0 6453 4091 4 (epub)

Contents

The events of 2020 have highlighted the critical need for leadership in all of our organisations. This book contains the perceptions, understandings and foresights shared by several global leaders and should benefit those who are interested in leadership for the 21st Century.

Foreword

A global pandemic, climate change, digital technologies, and rapidly changing geopolitics – there has never been a more important time for leadership. If we are to succeed in addressing such grand challenges, our leaders will need to embrace innovation and diversity, in all its forms, across every domain. This was my motivation, along with my wife Paula, for establishing the Andrew N. Liveris Academy for Innovation and Leadership at my alma mater, The University of Queensland.

It is my belief that, while great leaders can emerge naturally, if we invest in the skills and training of potential leaders, we create the opportunity to fast track their development. To ensure those emergent leaders develop a mindset that is future focused, and they are equipped to address what many are calling the greatest existential threats to humanity.

The Liveris Academy is developing a global talent pool of leaders. The curriculum provides high achieving undergraduate students with demonstrable leadership potential, a passion for sustainability and the opportunity to solve problems through large-scale innovation, thought leadership and collaboration.

During my career at Dow, I was fortunate to be exposed to a range of outstanding leaders who helped guide my own leadership journey. Several of these are featured in this book, and each chapter documents their interaction with the Liveris scholars. You will see from the informal Q&A style the level of insight they each provide as well as the ability of the Liveris scholars to draw out the key lessons they can take away from such engagement.

I am grateful we have been able to capture their experiences to share more widely through this book – *Developing our Leaders for this Century's Challenges*. It is the first of a series of leadership books – *Leadership for a Better Future*. Each year, we will feature a range of global leaders from across a diversity of sectors, cultures, and institutions.

I am delighted to introduce you to each of the authors and to share just some of the reasons why I hold them in such high regard.

We start with Ajay Banga, former CEO and current chairman of Mastercard. Ajay and I were true partners in our beliefs, our international perspectives, and the shedding of egos in our roles. Ajay is always direct and to the point, logical and pragmatic. Never confrontational, but firm in his mastery of his subjects and his passions. A true practitioner of diplomacy at the intersection of business and society.

Next, Paul Polman, former CEO of Unilever, lives and breathes passion and purpose. Evangelical in his beliefs that humanity needs to care about each other and the planet. Paul walks the talk in all his public and private personas. A true comrade-in-arms in the war against greed and making

Acknowledgement of Country

The University of Queensland (UQ) acknowledges the Traditional Owners and their custodianship of the lands on which we meet – the Jagera and Turrbal people. We pay our respects to their Ancestors and their descendants, who continue cultural and spiritual connections to Country. We recognise their valuable contributions to Australian and global society.

1

Introduction

Peta Ashworth & Alain de Sales

While the global pandemic has brought significant change and uncertainty, it is not the only event that has accentuated the need for new forms of leadership. The changing nature of geopolitics, trade relations, technological innovations and the ongoing impacts of climate change means that our future leaders need to be equipped with a different set of skills that allow them to address the unique challenges the 21st century will undoubtedly bring. However, there are some traditional leadership underpinnings that transcend through time, and this is the focus of this book.

Using a fireside chat format, delivered exclusively to the Andrew N. Liveris Academy for Innovation and Leadership scholars and staff at the University of Queensland, we present raw and personal insights from several prominent leaders of today. Humble, empathetic, and respectful. While these leaders acknowledge the importance of working collaboratively, in direct contrast to Surowiecki's *Wisdom of the Crowds*,[1] they exude a clarity, strength, and determination in their individual decision-making and leadership styles. A wisdom that is inspirational and engaging. Built not only on the vast experience of their entire careers but also from those who worked with them. Leaders who embrace diversity and inclusion through the wisdom of their teams, boards, cultures, genders, industries and more.

When discussing the strategies to improve leadership for the future, this book also subscribes to Infosys Chairperson N.R. Narayana Murthy's philosophy that "*Thirty percent of participants in any strategy discussion should be younger than age 30, because they are not wedded to the past.*"[2] In doing so, the Liveris scholars' unfettered and non-traditional critical thinking has been captured. All questions emerging from the scholars highlight areas of interest aimed at young and potential leaders. The perceptions, understandings and foresights shared through the interaction between these experienced global leaders and emerging ones are in a league of their own. It is something that anyone with an interest in leadership for a better future will surely benefit from and hopefully inspire them to 'do good by doing well'. To augment the discussion, each chapter in the book ends with a succinct reflection from one of the scholars to encapsulate their learning from the interaction with the leader.

1 James Surowiecki, *The Wisdom of Crowds: Why the Many Are Smarter Than the Few and How Collective Wisdom Shapes Business, Economies, Societies, and Nations* (New York: Doubleday, 2004).

2 Vijay Govindarajan and Chris Trimble, "The CEO's Role in Business Model Reinvention," *Harvard Business Review*, January-February, 2011, https://hbr.org/2011/01/the-ceos-role-in-business-model-reinvention.

she emphasises the need to focus equally on the R and the D – particularly the commercialisation of research. And on artificial intelligence (AI), cautions that as a reflection of humanity can be used for good and bad. It is here again Rometty emphasises the importance of ethics and trust to ensure that AI will be used for good and the opportunities it brings to the future of work. Her two leadership lessons: (1) only you define who you are; and (2) be honest with people and paint reality, but always give hope in that context.

In Chapter 6, we hear from Sharan Burrow, general secretary of the International Trade Union Confederation (ITUC). Sharan's focus is on ensuring fairness and equity in the global workforce. The statistics she cites provides sobering insights into the state of the world's employment, emphasising how the social contract today is broken and exacerbated further by the COVID-19 pandemic. Sharan reports, in 2020 alone, the pandemic resulted in a loss of 250 million jobs, with at least a further 130 million jobs at risk in 2021. With less than 50% of the global workforce employed in democratic countries and over 60% of the world's labour force working in informal work – no minimum wage, no rule of law, no social protection – it is daunting to consider how to enact change. Fortunately, Sharan provides a clear framework of where the focus should be. Her four pillars she introduces provides hope that together we can build an inclusive future that ensures greater equality and shared prosperity for all.

The last leader in this series is Dr Alan Finkel, former Chief Scientist of Australia. Finkel's early advice is not to sit around waiting for things to happen, if you wish to make a difference, you need to be active to be seen and heard. Throughout the chapter, you can hear Finkel's clear passion for science. He emphasises the need for evidence-based policymaking and how a clear and enthusiastic message goes a long way in gaining necessary support for sound scientific ideas. Another insight from Finkel is the importance as a leader to not just communicate a vision but also be involved in operationalising the idea to make it happen. Finkel also touches on the importance of government, industry and science working together to create improved outcomes for all. He touches on the impact of the collegiate approach in the early days of COVID-19 National Cabinet, which brought about a bi-partisan approach to addressing issues. Having completed the Finkel Review to develop a blueprint for Australia's electricity market, the National Hydrogen Strategy and the Low Emission Technology Roadmap, Finkel finishes by providing his own insights how Australia is addressing climate change and how to reduce emissions while allowing society to prosper.

Reflecting across each of the chapters, there are some common themes that fall out. Most significant is the humility of each of the leaders, despite their positions of influence across the world. Their lives as leaders appear to be cemented in the importance of values; being strong enough to make the hard decisions; but also open to the voices and advice of others – either internal or external to their organisations. Despite the changing nature of the world we are living in, these leaders provide hope that we can find a way forward that reduces inequity and celebrates diversity, at the same time recognising there is always a touch of serendipity – being in the right place at the right time – that can help to influence outcomes. However, they make it clear that it is important for leaders to lead by example and be across the operational details of the organisations they lead. We hope you will all gain some inspiration from reading this book. It has been an absolute pleasure to work with each of these influential leaders and their teams to bring this to you. Enjoy.

2

Leadership in the 21st Century

Andrew Liveris

13th July 2020

Globalisation, unfortunately, has been fuelled off the back of three or four decades of massive expansion of the Chinese economy and has come at the price of some pretty big, important topics of the geopolitical kind – notably climate change. But not just climate change, how we're all reacting to this pandemic is another good example of globalisation not working.

There are trade issues and others that are coming because of geopolitical failure and loss of faith in working together internationally and globally. Well before COVID-19, multilateralism itself was a failing statecraft, and unilateralism was becoming topic du jour, which is rather than work in global harmony, I'm going to work by working with individual nations, so one-on-one agreements. If you look at global institutions, whether it be the

United Nations or the World Health Organisation (WHO) in current circumstances, or the World Trade Organisation (WTO) as it relates to the trade issues, and so on, they're all not working. And in fact, even the funding models of things like the International Monetary Fund and the World Bank are not working either.

The need to rescue economies is now becoming quite common. The way the rescue is occurring is actually to do the only thing that governments seem to be able to do with some degree of harmony, which is to print money. In fact, the printing of money and the piling up of debt on the public sector side is escalating. And right now, quite concerningly as it relates to fixing the COVID-19 issues, a lack of courage in fiscal policy has come because of the tectonic shift in the way we account for profit.

Profit of the bottom-line kind – and certainly with public listed enterprises, but even the private enterprises such as private equity companies – has been more about profit in the near term, and no view towards the longer term in terms of investment. And, in fact, as a CEO, as I did for 14 and a half years, I often recount to my friends at the non government organisations (NGOs) or to institutions I belong to right now, and I belonged to while I was a CEO, like Richard Branson's B Team, I would tell them that in that entire time as CEO I don't remember one earnings call. I don't remember one interaction with any financial analyst that belonged to any of our institutions that owned our company, ever asking me about environmental, social and governance (ESG) factors.

Not once! Not a single financial analyst ever asked me about the topic of climate change or topic of pandemics or the topic of a social licence to operate. Social licence to operate is an issue that is driven by public policy interacting with private sector. It is the enormous gap that I see in the development of the new global order in the digital world. The arrival of digital itself is creating its own set of problems from privacy issues, to cyber issues, to conduct issues, to frankly the living-in-the-moment issue.

The distracting orientation of tools like Instagram and Facebook and the like, are defining a new reality for most people. Versus people really wanting to study and educate and do the detailed understanding of the content, before they walk through the context. In fact, the political rhetoric seems to live in trying to grab the eyeballs, trying to grab the headlines versus the definition of policy.

Policy evaporating from politics is now almost a fixed event. In other words, people don't get elected based on good policies, they get elected based on good politics. So he or she who yells the loudest, he or she who raises the most money, he or she who actually has the most influence over groups, he or she that actually can engender fear and emotion, has a better chance of getting elected than the person who has the thoughtful approach to answers for fiscal policy.

We have to find solutions to these complex problems and I really believe that the generation that you lead, can lead and will lead has a responsibility working with our generation to lay out a pathway where you can contribute. And certainly I'll play my part, as I've already demonstrated that I'm very keen to do. This will be done in both the public setting and the private setting, in creating the new alliances that need to be struck, to create more medium- to long-term investment.

We need inclusive capitalism to become the norm. We need our metrics to measure the success of what is profit, to include not just ESG factors, but societal factors. We need to bring the word 'equality' into the boardrooms, and into management as a measurement tool, not as narratives and rhetoric. We need to not just be inflamed in the moment and then forget it the next moment as the next thing arrives, but actually have accountability through a whole generation of people who hold others to account.

The methods I've seen that have done that successfully elsewhere have responsible government being met by responsible society, being met by responsible publicly-listed corporations or private sector corporations. I do think we're seeing a generation of that sort of leader emerge in both the political arena and also in the business arena. I do see the Marc Benioffs, even here in Australia, with the Scott Farquhars and the Mike Cannon-Brookes and the Eytan Lenkos starting to appear.

My only word of caution for all of you is, as every pendulum swings, don't swing too far in the wrong direction. I think pendulums do swing, but they always find equilibrium. I think what we're seeking is a new equilibrium. We have dis-equilibrium based on the past. We now need to create a new equilibrium. And yes, over-correcting is part of that. But recognise it for what it is. It's an over correction, rather than staying in that place which creates a new instability. That to me means we've got to do more listening than talking. We've got to do more understanding than lecturing, and we've actually got to create literacy in the public-private interface, which is what I hope the Academy seeks to do, and of course your participation in it is a very vital part of it.

What leadership lesson have you learnt really early in your career and how did that impact how you grew as a leader throughout your career? – *Scholar, Javan McGuckin*

Without suggesting I'm some sort of mutation, which I sometimes think I am, I just very early on developed an incredible impatience with things that I didn't understand. So the very early lessons I learnt, was when I wasn't understanding something, rather than just actually say I didn't understand it, I sought to understand. Which meant that I networked like crazy. I figured out where to go to get answers. And the straight-line way of doing that is within your environment, right?

But I got uncomfortable – I got comfortable being uncomfortable. I would go to the adversarial voice. In other words, if I didn't understand why people thought pesticides were bad, I would go and listen to the people who thought pesticides were bad and try to understand their point of view. And then I would go seek to find answers to what they were asking, and then bridge-build that through. Look, here is what they say, here is what you say. Here is a way of looking at it.

Whether you're right or wrong, doesn't really matter. What matters is we both understand the positions. Let's find some solutions. A solution mindset versus a problem amplification mindset is something I had early on that I kept applying to whatever job I was given. So networking to get the right answers, or at least answers that I needed to get that weren't in my purview, and then finding a way to integrate them into some proposed path forward, meant I was willing to take a risk, a personal risk.

You could look pretty dumb to some people when you're asking some pretty dumb questions, but what you find out is no one is asking that question. So, I guess I'll wrap up my answer by saying, seeking to simplify versus making things more complex, I think is a leadership attribute that can be learnt. And that's something that I would say I learnt very early on.

Given motivation is a prevalent issue at the moment, not just with Coronavirus, but also with this age of social media and the technology that we're going into, how do you find the motivation to undertake the numerous things in your bio, and how do you know when to step back and not take on more? – *Scholar, Simeon Gover*

Well again, and I answered the previous question by starting out saying I'm not a mutation, I might actually have to profess that I might be. Look, I'm just interested in so many things. I rarely find something I'm not interested in. And I learnt early on, rather than trying to control that – maybe the mutation piece that has a lot of energy and I don't know how to stop – maybe that is a mutation, I don't know. But the energy I have, I try to focus it on the topics I'm most interested in. I can't narrow it easily. So then I find their intersections. I mentioned one in my opening remarks. I mean, I could have stayed a private sector, public company CEO, live in my bubble, and made success happen. But I wasn't interested in just doing that. I was interested in that intersection with the public sector and in particular government.

And, for me, government was infuriating. And when I talk about my current remit with the Australian Government and what I'm doing to help this government, our governments, it's very infuriating to me to see people who are paid a lot of money – maybe not huge amounts of money, but they're paid a lot of money – being comfortable in keeping the status quo. So I can't not be interested in helping them change that. And many people said, "What are you trying to do? You can't change it?" And I said, "Yes, I can. Yes, I can. I can."

If it's just me, if I'm an army of one, then I'll count success, because I've changed one person. And if I'm lucky, two. And then they might change three or four. So that amplification, that keeps me going on many things. But I work at the intersections for synergies. I try to find positive synergies. So getting specific, this country has a failed energy policy. Now, a country as smart as this one should have a winning energy policy. Now, so far, none of you listening to this will disagree with that, right? So it isn't the direction that's being challenged. It's not even the what – what are the components of that. It's the how.

How to get energy policy done. And so what you've got to do is put your energy into helping the who, do the what, to go where, by showing them how. And as the years go by, and as it did in my career, I fundamentally made a living out of showing people how to do something. Because the intellect on the where and the what and even the who was not actually the issue. I've often worked with people much smarter than me, but they didn't know how. So that keeps me going. And, frankly, yeah, I'm probably overbooked, but I'm okay with that. And, yeah, I'm probably working too many hours a day. And, yeah, I probably have made – I don't know – a joke out of the word 'retirement'. I was never going to retire anyway. But, I mean, by getting my passions across multiple areas and then putting purpose and focus and finding out solutions actually, frankly, is my drug of choice.

In finding those adversarial voices, how do you actually specifically go out and become accountable and educated about those perspectives, when you're so involved in this sphere of people who think a certain way? – *Scholar, Lilly Van Gilst*

I think most of the adversarial forces do want outreach. They don't want to be just yelling, or saying you're an idiot, which sometimes they do. They actually do want outreach. And they particularly want outreach from the people they're attacking. They want someone to say, "Just a second, I really don't understand this. Explain to me why you want to ban plastics?" In a way, this can be a small victory, or maybe a large victory.

Sometimes people say to me, "Well, you're the king of plastics or you were the king of plastics, you're the enemy.

Why should I explain it to you?" In this instance, it is because I can actually help fix it. Those adversarial people will need to define exactly what their issue is with plastics. Because I can't believe for a second that their narrative is to eliminate all plastics. Because if they want to do that, they will want to wind back 200 years of human progress and live like we did 200 years ago, with a lifespan of age 40. That may be a choice they want to make but I'm pretty sure most of humanity doesn't want to make that choice.

So let's find a solution that actually speaks to what particular topic they're criticising people like me on. And so, they can't argue with that. Then they go into the difference between PT, PE, HDP, PP, ABS, PC, ETP and all the other polymers known to humankind. I'm sure the chemical engineers or chemistry majors will understand what I've just said. In response, I then explain all the differences in polymers to them.

Then they say, "Oh, yeah, you're right. I want to eliminate that plastic and this plastic. And, oh, by the way, I really want to understand nanoplastics, as it goes into the oceans." Well, then they aren't talking about any of those plastics. They're actually talking about detergents and how we wash clothes, and how we've got to do closed-loop washing cycles with no water being emitted. Now, if I've educated an adversary's view on the topic of nanoplastics in the ocean just now, that's because I've first sought to understand their view on what exactly they're worrying about. And actually, I worry about it too, because I don't want those nanoparticles in the fish I eat either. I'm a human.

So by showing my humanity, I'm not criticising them

for their positions, I'm actually building a bridge. And by seeking that out, you'd be surprised how many people don't know how to build. It's what Jim Collins wrote about – his book is getting a little more publicity again lately, *Good to Great* – the power of 'and' versus the tyranny of 'or'. 'And' is a powerful word. I want my modern lifestyle and I want social and environmental responsibility. Now if I put that word 'and' in there, you've got to get all the groups together. You can't have regulator and 'regulatee'. You can't have criticiser and the person being criticised in different camps. You've got to bring them together. This is the skill I want you all to adopt. You are the integrators for this century. You've got to create a people integration, systems integration, human activity that actually replaces what we've had. And this particular skill, I think, is one of the key skills that I hope you can pick up as you exercise your career.

> **You spoke a bit earlier about how hard you work, obviously, and you love your work, but throughout your career how did you go about maintaining an appropriate work-life balance? – *Scholar, Flynn Pearman***

When I was at Dow I used to get this question at my Town Halls with our people around the world an awful lot. And this new century of ours, this new humanity that we are all living, the pandemic is reminding us of the power of community, and the power of relying on each other. And I see it as a positive of COVID-19, actually. And even doing calls like this, I mean, I'd much rather do it in person, but we're connecting with each other using technology like never before and building our community. I used to answer the question on work-life balance by saying the word 'balance' is a terrible word because it implies an 'or'.

In actuality, you've got to get work-life integration, which is an 'and'. This means you need a community – and of course when people think community the most immediate way you think about community is your immediate family, your partner, spouse, children, if you have them along the way. You've got to get that community, which is the most important community of them all, to understand that the pathway you're on is their pathway as well. And that when they're little they pretty much don't have a choice, and I certainly now get that feedback back from my 20-somethings and 30-somethings. You know, why did we move so much? And the answer is, well, we moved so you could actually be multicultural. Because they are multicultural.

A lot of you would like to be multicultural, in fact probably a lot of you are. But I go to the positive of why rather than the negative, even now. The balance when you are little is not available. The integration is not available. But to your partner, integration is everything. So Paula and I, we were a team all the way through it. We could never not be a team. In fact, if we weren't a team, either one of us would have failed, maybe both. And I think this discussion extends beyond just your immediate family. It obviously goes to your first ecosystem of friends and maintaining those friendships along the way so that you can always have safe harbour.

I'm a great believer that we all need safe harbour. We all need safe harbour in the modern world, some people call that therapy sessions and going to psychiatrists. I think you create your own safe harbours by having loyalty, dependency, and people you trust along the way. And I have exercised that along the way. So in dark times, in times when I was going through tough times, you wouldn't want to trouble your immediate – in my case wife – partner, with that burden, especially if it was a work burden. The last thing you want to do is bring the burdens home. And I was lucky, I had a stay-at-home partner – my wife worked at home, she operated the family in all these different countries. But the last thing she needed was to hear my work burden, but I had a burden, and I needed to create an outlet.

So these safe harbours along the way allowed me to integrate myself with my humanity around me that I trusted. I did that when I first became CEO. I actually didn't know the CEO community very well, and I went and interviewed 20 successful CEOs. From those 20, you actually are talking to one of them this week – Paul Polman and I were friends first, CEOs second. I trust him and I would talk to him about things that I needed to talk to someone about. But if I showed vulnerability to pretty much anyone else, it would have shown weakness. And of course that's not a great model, because we all have weaknesses, but you've got to be careful with that, because you're leading.

So what I'm saying to you is integrating your life into your purpose and your passion is the only solution we have to the 24-hour conundrum. I mean, one of these days someone is going to find more time in the day. I don't know if that's even feasible, but the people who follow 'multiverses' say maybe that it is. But until we do, that 24-hour thing is pretty real. Now, of course, the other thing I mentioned, I don't need a lot of sleep, and I've proven that to myself even in retirement. I still get up early and go to bed late. So maybe that's a bit of it too. But I choose to be on Zoom calls at midnight tonight, helping the Kingdom of Saudi Arabia go through its current crisis. I choose that. I can say no. I choose it because I believe in it, and I am passionate about it. And at midnight my wife is asleep anyway, so it doesn't matter. But what I'm saying is, I am immersed in what I do, and the people around me were immersed with me in the ways I've described.

> **Was there a specific point in your career where you realised you wanted to make a major difference to sustainability and politics and manufacturing? – *Scholar, Esandi Kalugalage***

I entered my university life at The University of Queensland (UQ), and even my high school life – my last year was at State High, and even my time at Darwin High – always doing well on the academic side. What I kept getting, but never really believed about myself, was that my value system was derived from my community. I think I learnt this in spades when I got some accountability at Dow, and when I started really learning some things that mattered, such as the topics you raised.

What I didn't know is how much of my persona had a value system built into me from my being raised the way I was raised. And in an ethnic community – and those of you with ethnic backgrounds would identify with what I am about to say – I mean, ethnic communities can be really good and can be really bad. Because every time you move, the whole community knows what you're doing, and if you're a standout – success has many fathers and mothers and failure is an orphan. So suddenly I had many people claiming my success, but they had nothing to do with it.

At the same time, you realise there's a value system, which I've already described in the word 'community', that I had early. Which made me respect others, which made me a good listener and really made me – maybe through some of my own natural attributes – want to learn, which then made me curious. When I looked at joining Dow – I used the pesticide example before. For those of you who don't know this part of my student life, as a student, I was an avid protestor against Dow, because of the Vietnam War and napalm. I had long hair and I could show you pictures from that time, but I don't think I want to. I was part of that student protest movement. I also rallied against them on chlorpyrifos and pesticides and yet I took an interview with them.

Besides Dow, I also took interviews with DuPont and ICI and Esso and Shell and all those bad companies. I took an interview because I was forthright. I said, if I join you, what about this pesticide thing? Tell me about why we're eating pesticides. And the people interviewing me had to present the value system of the company. I did this while I was at Dow. I made sure whoever we sent to interview graduates or industry hires did not have the transactional answer. And this part of me that wanted to understand why an organisation was portrayed badly, I could seek answers from those organisations. And on the pesticide issue, it was borne of having the whole value system around the environment. And then some of the leadership positions Dow took from the attacks by the Environmental Protection Agency (EPA) in the 70s, I joined at that period of time. I saw the morphing of Dow go from, basically, the Ds, right. The first was 'denial'. Then the second was 'defence'. So those were two bad reactions to the term 'environmental', right? But I was of the camp saying we can't deny, we can't just defend, we have to go to the third D, which is 'discuss', and then go to the fourth D, based on science, 'debate'. And I was a leader in Dow doing those things through my management ranks. I would do that when I was a junior manager, while I was an engineer. I didn't do that just when I became CEO.

It was instilled in me, that our value system meant that Dow had to grow into this world that had actually grown around us while we were denying and defending it. And then finally when I became CEO, I said, "Okay, we've done a lot of debate and discussion, let's go and just do things now. Let's change our company." That progression through the Ds took Dow two-and-a-half decades. We don't have that luxury anymore. This digital world means the judge, jury, and in fact the people who are working for you judge you in the second, in the minute. Reputation, decades to earn, minutes to lose, is the way the world has evolved. So short cycle decision-making on a moving topic like environment, short cycle response curves out of things like manufacturing, is something I learnt along the way.

I was so frustrated when I wrote the book *Make It In America*, because politics had departed from policy on the vitality of the manufacturing ecosystem for the new century. Not the last century, not the smokestacks, not the textile looms, but digitised manufacturing, automation, sustainable manufacturing, the right to invent and innovate off the shop floor based on new technologies. That movement had not occurred in the US and all because of policy failure, and the Asian competitors had basically started to take all the market share on the new technologies for this century for humanity to function. So it was that recognition.

And I recognised it early in my career, that I could come into a company like Dow. Dow's great attribute – and frankly, I think this is an American company thing – still to this day is, it allowed you to have a voice, no matter where you were in the organisation. And I think whoever you join, or whatever you end up doing – and some of you may go the entrepreneurial route. People say what would you have done if you could go back and redo everything that you did, what would you do differently? I said I didn't realise it in myself, but I was an entrepreneur before that term became known. I probably would become an entrepreneur. I still want people like you to join a Dow and a DuPont and get that experience, but what I'm saying to you is, it wasn't available to people like me, so I made it happen inside the corporation and I got rewarded for it. Which to me was the big tick of the box on Dow's management value system.

What approaches are you and the rest of the National COVID-19 Coordination Commission team applying to maintain that positive relationship between the

private and the public sectors, and especially with regards to restarting the economy, a stage a lot of states are getting to now? – *Scholar, Victoria Barnes*

It's a great question, I have been really seconded. I'm an easy target, I'm a volunteer that's willing. And as people around me will currently note, I have been consumed with your question. And I would say I'm really encouraged by the development of two things in Australia and Australian politics that frankly I didn't expect to see after spending 20 years trying to get a couple of things like this started, but I am now seeing them three or four months in.

First, the crisis of the pandemic and the view to an economic recovery. As we see the second outbreak in Melbourne and Victoria, as we see even today's news of the hotel in Sydney, I wrote an op-ed a few weeks ago about how I don't think the recovery will occur until 2024, 2025. I'm normally an avid, unbridled, enthusiastic optimist. So if I say that, okay, that actually speaks to a few years where the answer to your question is in the unknowable. The two things I'm seeing that are coming out of the crisis that I was actually hoping to see, and I definitely can confirm to you that I'm seeing them, is a national coordination that's top down, that is not typical of the Australian democracy.

Now, the Australian democracy, the Westminster system, really doesn't work well on a planning horizon. And Australia is very unusual, because the two major parties, the Labor Party and the Liberal and National Coalition, are still closer to the centre than pretty much any other democracy around the world. What you've seen around the world – and the United States is a great example – is the Democrats have gone more left, and the Republicans have disappeared and have been taken over by something called the 'far right' or otherwise known as the Trump Party. There is no Republican Party left.

So this notion of schism and difference on solutions of the national kind – democracies have to function in those crises, and the way our government has chosen to respond is exemplary. It's creating a national cabinet and putting together the state premiers and the federal leaders, and doing it on a regular drumbeat, and then chunking the response into its pieces. Short-term, the actual health crisis and the supply chain interruptions that occurred. Medium term, which is the stuff I'm working on is, what parts of the economy do we need to build from here, what policies do we need to build them, and what 21st century toolbox do we apply to them? And then to do it with a view to not being re-elected. These are policies that are required by the nation. Nation first. Politics second. So check. I mean, very encouraging.

Second, in your question, you implied this point: the sheer creation of the National Commission is a public-private partnership. I've been screaming from the rooftops for one of those in Australia for two decades. I mean, not that the private sector has all the answers, but I guarantee you – and especially after my last four months – they have different answers than what Canberra does. And different from what each other state capital has. The civil service in Australia has a potent strength for continuity. It's a weak piece of government, in terms of change. They don't like change.

After spending 15 years changing Dow, I've got to tell you most people don't. Most people – to quote the American expression – don't like their cheese moved. So moving one's cheese in this crisis, with this burning platform, the civil service is having to respond and the private sector is getting a voice. Now, organising the private sector is the proverbial herding cats, okay. Because the private sector has all their different sectors, right, banking, tourism, etc. But, okay, some are like me, and people who have been around the block a few times, we've got some experience in doing this. I did it under Obama, I did it under Trump. If I can do it under two different presidents like that, I can certainly give it a shot here.

That's what Nev Power (Chief of the National COVID-19 Coordination Commission) and the Commission are doing, working with me on the manufacturing side. So those two things should lead to a game plan for economic recovery that should give you and your cohort, but most importantly, the unemployed and dis-employed Australians hope that there are jobs on the other side of the short-term issue. And the short-term issues, of course, are in the news every day, which is how to fix it with handouts. In essence, you know, JobSeeker, JobKeeper, all those programs, are to tide people over until that national recovery plan can be put in place and also the policies.

Focusing on government regulation and its role in facilitating business, how we can make it more effective in balancing the interests of business communities and the environment. How can

> **government and industries play an active part in shaping and streamlining green tape and red tape processes, so that business are better able to operate while still upholding principles of sustainability? – *Scholar, Megan Jones***

I have a recent specific example of that. Those of you who don't subscribe to the *Northern Territory News*, which I'm pretty sure is most of you, if not all of you, would not have noticed that I was on the front page of the *Northern Territory News* recently. My mates up there joke that I displaced the crocodile. There's always a crocodile on the front page of the *Northern Territory News*. So I was the crocodile on the front page. And it had portrayed me as a pro-fracking guy, based on some interview that I had done recently. And in the discussion – it was a political rhetoric, there's an election there next month – so the party that's anti-fracking portrayed me as the Darth Vader of the discussion. So I did a follow-up interview where I answered the question you asked.

I'm not anti-regulation, I am not pro-regulation, but I am for smart regulation. The word 'smart' in front of the word 'regulation' means you have a triangle to actually work with. Typically, governments don't work with that triangle. One is the regulator, the regulated, and the third is the people who give you the licence to operate, i.e., society. And that triangle needs all the facts presented to get the smart regulation.

Where do you get the facts? Well, the regulated, i.e., industry – in this case the oil and gas industry – will give you a lot of facts. But you will look at them with a raised eyebrow, because you'd say, well, you know, they're biased. I can't trust their data. They want to make money. They're evil empire people. So, fine. And there may be some companies out there like that. In fact, I daresay there are. So you must get the body of science that supports the topic, and the plus and minus of it, and you surround it with facts.

The regulator has a job. They need to get third-party verification of their position and there are plenty of people who will give you independent, third-party, auditable views on whatever you're regulating. How many pesticides, the topic of fracking – you need to get third party reviews of those. Most of these are done by proof points, so not just mathematical or scientific theory, demonstrable proof points of environmental standards elsewhere. With fracking, there's a plethora of that available from the United States' experience, but not just the United States, there is also the United Kingdom, Argentina and Germany. There are pros and cons for each issue. There is the water table issue; the type of fracking; the type of chemical you use; how the land gets treated and rehabilitated. As well as how the landowner gets to take part in the economic system that is created. All of that needs to be looked at from a third-party viewpoint.

Then of course you need to go through the third leg of the triangle which is public submission. The public has views and you've got to lay it all out on the table. Going back to the topic on the front-page headline, if you say the Beetaloo Basin may get developed. To find out if the development goes forward, we must use all those processes I mentioned earlier. So the regulated and regulator need to present the right regulation to the local population. If the Indigenous people living there don't take part in the economic benefit correctly, so they can actually do it according to their societal norms – that is, what they want for their people not what we want for them – if we don't get that licence from the local population, then the other two shouldn't act independently. Now that triangle is smart regulation. That's what we suggested in the United States, under Obama. That's what, in essence, has been put in place, even under Trump. Because what ends up happening is you actually can't find a fault in that discussion. Now, if you have regulations being born in isolation, which you have in this country, with smart people sitting in rooms in Canberra or Brisbane or somewhere, writing with their great legal briefs, massive regulations based on independent studies they've done through some research. This then gets passed into law, and suddenly the 'regulated' wakes up one day and says, oh, just a second, you're going to crush my industry with this expense or cost, and you're going to lose all those jobs. Or you're not attracting foreign investment because you're not an easy place to do business.

For instance, there's been a project in Western Australia that is in its twelfth year. The proponents of that project have gone through six ownership changes. The original sponsors of that project were a foreign company that gave up. So that's hardly efficient government. America put in place something called SelectUSA, based on our recommendations. SelectUSA takes every investment proposal, puts them through the machinery I just discussed, and has an answer in 30 days. Greece has done it. Australia is number 59 on the economic complexity scale. You don't want to be that number. You don't want to be out of the top 10, let alone number 59. Just ahead of us (Australia) is Senegal, and just behind us is Zimbabwe. Are you serious? This is what the collective smarts of this country have developed. We make the TV show *Yes Minister* look like a reality show. And for those of you who are too young to know what *Yes Minister* is, go YouTube it, and you'll see what I'm talking about. Anyway, this is a passionate area for me.

Could you further expand on what additional steps you feel the Australian Government should take to prioritise sustainability? – *Scholar, Amber Spurway*

Well, my view is the word 'sustainability' needs to stop being a noun. It needs to become an adjective. And frankly, it needs to disappear, because this country should have the highest standard in the world, in terms of quality of life. And to do that – and ask Paul Polman this, because he's a champion in this area – we need to integrate the value of nature into all of our decision-making. See, nature has a value. Nature is finite. Again, unless we have a mysterious extra dimension I talked about earlier, or if we go to Elon Musk's populate Mars plan. We only have this planet to work with and this planet has an ecosystem that's finite, and we abuse it.

We abuse it, because when we put things on it, in the name of humanity, we don't price it properly. We don't price to replace it, and we certainly don't price it globally. So we can get abuse in emerging countries, because they will argue, hey, just because you made mistakes deforesting most of America, don't stop us deforesting Africa, or deforesting the Amazon. We need arable land. Do you know, as we sit here today, Africa is technically out of arable land. There's no arable land in Africa. So what they've got to do is tear down jungles and tear down forests and basically put herds of cattle and others – proteins – on the land, which of course threatens all the wildlife of Africa.

Actually, our responsibility is to make sustainability a part of, and integrate it into, our economic decisions. Unfortunately, we've allowed the greed gene to overcome our decision-making. I have railed against this and I am currently writing my second book which says inclusive capitalism has to change with our owners. Financial institutions do not measure us on ESG factors. They say they do. Maybe one or two percent of the money in the world does that. Until it's a significant percent – 30, 40, or 50% – public corporations won't change their behaviours unless they actually see an economic proposition. At Dow, I introduced pricing the value of nature around us – air, land, water, etc. – into every factory decision, every building decision, accordingly. That changed the way we did projects.

Inside Dow we have a price on carbon. That changes how we do projects. So you have a dozen or so corporations, maybe two dozen by now, read the announcement from the CEO of Danone, just recently, Emmanuel Faber, and how he's received the first French licence to be what the US is calling a B Corp. B Corps are the way of the future, because they will make sustainability integrated into their economic decisions. Now, that's the company response.

The government response is way, way more important, actually. Because regulatory standards need to be adopted for the future, rather than look back to the past. How we talk about things like deforestation, water management for drought and wildfires, and carbon need to be integrated into our policy frameworks. This will then engender an invention innovation engine to make all that happen technologically. One begets the other.

Right now we're getting into renewables and all that through the worst of all worlds which is subsidy, and then the removal of subsidy. Germany has just done that. You can't do it that way. Business will never invest against that. Government will invest against it and lose money. So you've got to integrate it. And it's a very important question you're asking. Again, what you learn here is that this is a leadership issue, big time. And frankly, it needs loud voices from society.

What an average day is like for you? – *Scholar, James Orman*

Wow. I think I saw that question and I was hoping it would never get asked. On average, I try to do some exercise in the morning. I'm usually good at that. I then have a coffee, or maybe two, with my wife. But that's the only two I have all day. So if you think caffeine is driving this engine, it's partly true, but only in the mornings. Well, COVID-19 has changed everything, but unusually today, I'm actually in someone's building. Before this event I had an interview, which by the way will air on Sky News. I'm one of the people being interviewed on the American-Australian alliance, which we haven't touched on here.

So I'm in Sky's building. So unusually I'm in the city, but pretty much most of the time I'm operating from the back room of our apartment in the eastern suburbs of Sydney. I'll pop out and get a drink or have lunch if that is available. If it's not, I'll just plough through and surface at around 3–3.30 pm. My son and his wife and now grandson have been trapped in Sydney for the last three or four months, which I'm trying to make permanent, but I don't know how to do that. If you have any tips, let me know. But my wife and I try to see our grandson at least daily. And then I'll come back. We'll pretty much eat at home or maybe get a food delivery or something. And then I'll click back into phone calls, Saudi, US, somewhere around 9 or 9.30 pm, and some of them will stop at midnight, some will go to 1 or 2 am – tonight will be one of those. Tomorrow, my first is at 8 am, so I've got to start all that stuff earlier, like at 6 am. So is that too much for you? I probably inadequately answered that.

Scholar Reflection – Javan McGuckin

Upon coming to university, I thought that I knew what made a good leader. In my eyes it was simply someone who made the right decisions for the group and was able to instruct others on how to best achieve a goal. Now whilst this may not strictly be wrong, I feel my initial view did not capture the type of leaders we need today.

Our current leaders, across business, government, and NGOs, are tackling complex problems with no easy solution. These problems are typically not best solved through a single school of thought, instead they require a multidisciplinary approach. It is no easy feat to collaborate with people outside of our field, especially when their way of approaching a problem is so different to our own. This begs the question, what can young and emerging leaders do to effectively collaborate on solving these issues, and what will make them effective leaders?

The opportunities to engage with Andrew Liveris among other leaders has really driven home one key message, that leaders need to have a strong sense of personal values and ethics which they both stand behind and advocate for. These values and ethics should underpin our decision-making and be made clear to the teams we are working in.

Value based decision-making puts key priorities at the head of discussions and ensures that social justice and environmental issues are not treated as an afterthought. This was reflected in Andrew's comments on a business's social licence to operate. These comments expanded on the idea of doing well while doing what's right and that it is possible to achieve economic success without compromising on our morals.

For young and emerging leaders, it is important that we understand what is important to us and the values which we want to see reflected in our society. This will allow us to approach these complex problems with a guiding principle for the outcome we are aiming to achieve. These guiding values aid in multidisciplinary collaboration as it unites the team under a common goal and can be used to bridge differences in our approaches.

I'm thankful for this perspective which Andrew has exposed to the Liveris scholars, and I encourage our leaders, current and future, to carefully consider what values matter to them and to not compromise these when making tough decisions.

3

Creating a More Inclusive and Just Society Through Digitisation

Ajay Banga

14th July 2020

Looking back now over 30-odd years of working, the number one factor I feel very good about is that I allowed serendipity to drive my career, and I didn't overthink this or over-plan it or over-process it. That serendipity allows you to flow with the tide a little bit. Serendipity allows you to seize opportunities when they are presented to you, and that allows you to take the risks that those opportunities represent. That is important, and I think a lot of young people today over-plan and over-think through their options. For example, thinking, "Hey, I'm joining this company, I'd like to be 'that' 10 years from now."

The one thing you know for sure is that structure would have changed by the time your 10 years are done, and that job would probably have disappeared or been changed completely, and therefore planning for a job 10 years out is probably a waste of your time. What's more interesting is considering what experiences you like to have; what things you would like to be doing; what people would you like working with; who would you like to learn from; and what things do you want to get your hands dirty with? That's more fun, and if you do those, your breaks tend to come. So, I say serendipity ruled my life, and I plan to allow for that to continue.

The second factor that is interesting is that as you go higher in your career, you have a chance for your voice to be amplified many times by virtue of being the senior person. The higher you go, the greater the amplification, meaning if Andrew as the CEO of Dow Chemical used his bully pulpit to talk about something, it got multiplied many times over by employees and outsiders who were listening to him, and the same is true for me. You must use your voice wisely, because if you use it unwisely, you're wasting and dissipating the energy of the surrounding people.

Thus the second thing I did was to use my voice carefully. That said, I made mistakes while using my voice, but I've also done well with using my voice. I think the one thing I feel very good about in my voice is that I've made meaning out of standard phrases like 'you can do well by doing good'. I have proven in our company that you can do that. And I have led on financial inclusion around the world, making it a part of our business model. You can do well by doing good. I started out with a $20 billion market cap company that's now $300+ billion, depending on the day you look at the share price. I think if you can do that while attempting to get 500 million people out of financial exclusion into it, that is an achievement and shows you can lead with doing good.

The last factor is related to the concept of IQ. When we were young – I'm now 60, and Andrew and I have similar age profiles, although he thinks he looks younger and more handsome – we were told that IQ was everything. You have to be smart, you have to do well in college. Then somewhere along the way, we learnt that EQ mattered, because you're managing through difficult circumstances, so EQ became important. And I'm saying now that DQ matters, which is your 'decency quotient', which is leading with your innate human decency and care, kind of what Andrew typifies in his life. If you do that well, you're going to have a great time. I think I've brought DQ into the public space, and I talk about it with openness.

As I look back on those things – serendipity, taking things as they come, not over-planning, making sure that you lead with your heart, not just your mind, bringing both to work – it's all about being this decent person, living what today is called inclusive capitalism, which is doing well by doing good. Just live it, and it's a good way to go.

We're in the middle of this pandemic; in your view, did we see it coming, could we see it coming, and now that we're sitting here, what's the path that needs to be taken? All around the world, there's a similar pattern with lots of examples of what not to do and what do we need to do as a species, maybe you can share your perspective using DQ? – *Andrew Liveris*

Almost no one foresaw this pandemic coming. If you look at all disaster preparedness at senior government levels – you and I have been involved with the United States government for a while, you're active with your government of Australia as well. If you look at their paperwork, their documentation, their black swan scenarios, they've planned for everything but not this, which is interesting, given that we were all planning for biological warfare ever since terrorism exploded onto our shores. Effectively, while this is not biological warfare, the downstream impacts of it are pretty similar. And so you would have thought that we would have had scenarios planned that would allow for personal protective equipment, ventilators and related equipment. We expected science to have been invested in the quick development of antidotes to different diseases, like vaccines. But interestingly, I think everybody paid lip service to it. No one actually did enough in that space. Companies certainly did not, governments did not, and so I think we all failed in that form.

One thing we have learnt is the world is even more interconnected than we thought it was, because the prior occurrences of these viruses were mostly confined to regional places. For instance, Ebola never got out of a few countries in Africa. SARS, MERS, avian flu, also did not spread; while the latter did from mainland China and spread to some countries in the far east, they hardly went anywhere else. They went to the few countries, and they were contained and managed. What changed is that China became a much more important citizen of the world, and the number of Chinese people travelling overseas and the number of people travelling into China multiplied many times over the last decade between the avian flu and now. I think that changed the dynamic of the global spread completely. While America banned Chinese people from coming into our country, we didn't ban Europeans, and guess what, the virus was in Europe. And so if we look at the strains of Coronavirus in New York, it's the European strain that came in. The DNA testing is showing that this hit China, then to Europe and came from Europe into New York. It didn't come from China into New York. This tells you that in this deeply interconnected world, you can't put up enough barriers. Protectionism will not save you, 'precautionism' could. 'Precautionism' in virus terms is obvious, but in trade terms would say develop your local industry, develop your local capabilities, develop your local skills and talent, but don't for a minute believe you can shut the barriers of the country and somehow grow in this deeply interconnected world. And I think that's the biggest lesson we've all got.

Now, how do we come out of this? I've talked to investors and the board about how I think there are four stages for a company: containment, stabilisation, normalisation, and growth. Containment is the freefall when you shut everything down. Stabilisation is the bottom of that pyramid. Normalisation as you begin to come out of it and return to normal. But a lot of things don't come back to normal: long distance travel, mass entertainment and other similar elements – real growth is when these elements come back. I think they're mostly in some stage of normalisation across the world and you step back and forth, like we did in Victoria, or we did in Singapore, or we're doing in the south of the United States, but growth requires a vaccine. That's why we put all that money into a therapeutic accelerator earlier in the game to get research into a vaccine going with the Gates Foundation. I think growth requires a vaccine, and anybody who tells you the full, global distribution of a vaccine is three months away is a liar. To get this in size and scope and widely enough distributed to seven billion people is over three months away. Even if we can find one through accelerated testing, to get it out there at scale and to make sure that we don't have haves and have nots in the vaccine world, which I'm fearful of, you're going to have to allow this to play out over a period of time. You should be thinking about 2021 being the year the vaccine reaches out into people.

I am very interested in everything you've been saying about prosperity and inclusion and DQ. Were there any times in your career where you have had to overcome some sort of institutionalised opposition to your key values and your key ideas of decency, so you can work your way up to a place where you can have that amplification and make that positive change? – *Scholar, Lilly Van Gilst*

I think there are two questions inside that, question one is earlier in life, how did I manage to stay true to my values and build a coalition of the willing? The second part of the question is even when I am leading and I can actually push my point of view on people, did I still encounter conflict?

Let's take the first one first, about being true to my values earlier in my life. There are no shortcuts in this, and you will definitely encounter circumstances, leaders, bosses and others who will agree and disagree with what you think may constitute this high ideal that you're trying to live up to. Call it inclusive capitalism, call it decency, call it whatever you want; there are also lots of interpretations of those words and lots of value judgments in those words.

Value judgements create conflict, because the person above you will respond to that statement being, "Oh, you think I'm not doing this? Let me therefore poke you in the eye." And that's just a normal human reaction to feeling defensive about being questioned for what they thought was the right thing to be doing. It's not that most of them are not coming to work to be mean to you. People don't come to work to be mean to each other. People generally come to work to do the right thing, but they get misguided, they get taken in directions, they subscribe to a point of view and they get taken there. There's no shortcut. You should be prepared to fight for what you think is right. To explain, by fight I don't mean actually fight, I mean re-emerge as a merchant of peace and do it in a good way.

To be true to your values, you must win some and lose some. You become a better person for those you lose. Actually, if you win too many of them, then you will only get cocky and overconfident about how smart you are, and that's a problem in itself. So, think that you're going to win some and you're going to lose some, which is okay. Just stay true to yourself and your principles and try to keep taking people with you. When I was young and in business school, I was told that half your success comes from convincing your boss that you have a good idea. And the other half is the quality of the idea. I think in life we have many great ideas, but if we convince nobody, it's of no use. I think it's very much a part of how you convince people and how you take them with you, and so that's why communication and the ability to communicate with simplicity, passion and vision is such an important part of being a good leader, and somebody people will follow. That answers the first part of your question.

The second part, I think you will find many instances when people in the company who work for you, with embedded interests, who have been used to doing certain things in a certain way, will look upon you as being the agent of change that they wish would just die and disappear. There's nothing wrong with that. Again, it's human behaviour, it's the way people think. The trick is are you willing to come back to that topic enough times to say, "Let me explain why I think this is a good idea," and then celebrate the successes that you can get, so that you make examples out of those that work well, and do it in a nice way, in a constructive way.

The one thing I learnt is criticising will make sure that the conflict increases. Constructive criticism, on the other hand, will take many people with you. I'm not saying you hide from conflict, I'm just saying you manage it in a way that people feel they can win by following you, as compared to your way was the right way, and therefore mine was the wrong way. That right-wrong, black and white, is an awful place to be; that's the issue. Will you find conflict even when you're the boss? Absolutely, but if you can show the maturity to take them with you rather than force them to follow you, I think you'll enjoy your journey a great deal.

You know, there's an old saying that it's very lonely at the top, and in a way that is true, because when you're the CEO, even the people you were friendly with growing up in the company or in your business, they come to your room with an agenda. No one is coming to your room to hang out and shoot the breeze with you, because your damage potential is higher than your benefit potential when you're the CEO. When they come to your room they have an agenda, they're coming there to convince you to do something. It may not be a bad agenda, it's normally a good agenda, but it's an agenda. Therefore, it's lonely at the top if you start believing the agenda is all that matters. It's not lonely at the top if you take them with you. Then there's lots of people with you, and that constructive criticism will have taken people with you. That is the best way to reduce your loneliness and make it a fun journey.

You spoke before about the decency quotient, which is quite relevant in the current global economy for business leaders. I'm interested to know whether you think the decency quotient is something business leaders should possess inherently, or something that can be taught and changed? – ***Scholar, Esandi Kalugalage***

Well, I think values are something you get when you're young from your parents, school, environment, wider family and friends, and all those good things. I think values you do get, but I don't believe you can't learn things along the way from the mistakes and the twists and turns in your journey. To say that you don't learn things along the way would make you a very closed person and I don't believe people are closed. I think they're willing to listen if you make the effort to explain to them why it's important for them to understand that. I think that is an important angle in your life.

My belief is the decency quotient is really important. I believe that more people should embrace the idea of leading with decency, but I believe that the word 'decency' can get misconstrued very easily. So, let me take a minute to explain something about it. Decency does not mean that you must be nice to everybody, or that you must be kind to everybody every day. Actually, most people who work for you, what they really want is transparency and fairness, with clear guidelines on what they are doing well, and clear help to improve. Nobody is expecting to be told only good things about themselves all day long, because if you get only that, at some point you're going to stumble.

Most people expect you to be fair, but they expect you to be transparent, and in that process, you can give them hard feedback as well. There's nothing wrong with that. It's okay. But that decency is not kindness, it is fairness; it is transparency; it is a hand on your back, not a hand in your face; it's a level playing field. In this day and age of racial conversations in the US and several countries around the world, many people will bend in the opposite direction and say, "Let me just tick the box and appoint three African-American senior managers." That is nonsense. That's not decency, that is pandering. Because I look different from everybody else, but I want people to say I got my job because of my inherent capability and my self-worth, not because I look different.

All I want is a level playing field. You give me a level playing field, I will run to win. Now how do you get a level playing field? That's the science and the art, because very often, right from the beginning – from your education, from your childhood, your healthcare – the playing field has been stacked against you if you were unfortunate enough to be the wrong ethnicity, or the wrong gender, or the wrong sexual orientation. That needs fixing, do not get me wrong, it's hard work, but I don't want to be told that you did me a favour. I do not want to be told that I filled a box for you to tick; I'm not going to do that. I want to feel I got my job because of how good I am, and I led from the front with my skills and capabilities. So, decency, it can be very easily misinterpreted. It is meant to be straight down the middle, tough and soft at the same time. Life is a bundle of contradictions, and decency is contradictory in its nature. You need to be both. You need to be hard, but you need to be fair.

I really admire the selfless commitment that you have made towards making sure that everyone has a chance to get an identity, as well as the ability to loan money from a bank. My question is when did you first latch onto this idea and did you receive any backlash when you were trying to implement it? – *Scholar, Victoria Barnes*

I first latched onto it when working at Citibank. Citi had a really interesting employee called Bob Annibale. He used to be a trader once upon a time, and people say traders are greedy bums – Bob was a trader but he was a wonderful human being. In 1997, when I was working in London, Bob came to me while I was managing Central Europe, the Middle East and Africa. He said, "I believe that I can help in my trading desk to take small microcredit loans, $50 loans for women who run a little fishmonger or a newspaper business or who sell fruit. I can take those loans off the balance sheet of all these NGOs and free up their balance sheet to lend more. What's called 'securitisation' in the finance world, which is normally done only for big ticket loans, I can do it for the small ticket loans and enable the NGOs to lend much more."

I looked at Bob and said, "Why would you do that?" and he said, "Because I think it will make a difference," and I was cynical about it and I said, "Yeah, Bob, why don't you go away and come back when you've figured it out." He came back in three months' time. "I've figured it out and I'm going to do a tranche, and all I need is for you to sign off on the risk." I knew there was a catch, and I looked at the risk a little more carefully. Actually, it was a pretty minor risk, so I took the risk and signed off on it, and we did the first ever, in the world, microcredit securitisation for a Bangladeshi NGO called BRAC, which used to enable loans for women in Bangladesh.

Once we finished the securitisation, I must have got 20 phone calls from similar NGOs saying, "Oh my God, can you help us?" and I suddenly realised that getting access to capital was the single biggest problem for micro SMEs, for small SMEs, because they were outside the financial world in some never-never land where they operated in cash and borrowed money from moneylenders, not from real banks. Getting them into the financial mainstream would make a difference in their lives. Since most of them were women, they in turn would make a difference to the lives of their families.

I learnt by travelling to Bangladesh that this was a virtuous cycle when I actually saw the impact of what we were doing. That's what got it going. And I learnt that what locks them out of lending is being in the informal economy. Being in the informal economy is a product, firstly, of them not having an identity and therefore no bank will open an account for them. And second, by being out of the banking account system, they remain in the grey economy. You've got to break that logjam, and the first point to break the logjam is to give them an identity. And then the second point to break the logjam is to give them a loan safely, and at a fair price, and then you can start the cycle going. That's how it started. It goes back to 1996, 1997. I learnt a little bit – but I did very little other than ride on Bob Annibale's shoulders for a while, while Bob was doing all the hard work. Then somewhere in the early 2000s when I moved to the US, I actually got an opportunity to run microfinancing. Sandy Weill was the CEO and wanted someone to run this microfinancing business. I was sitting in the room and making noises about how I thought it was a very interesting business and he said, "Fine, why don't you run it?" And I said, "I am not so sure about that." And he said, "Well now, tag you're it." So I ended up with this business, and then one thing led to the other from there. Remember serendipity!

How does financial inclusion fit in with the transition towards a cashless society? – *Scholar, Flynn Pearman*

I do not know that cashless is the word. Less cash is a better word than cashless, but it sounds less cool, so most people convert it into cashless. I started out by saying 'kill cash'; that was my slogan. My corporate PR guy said that sounds awfully bad, so they came back with a more malleable statement, called cashless. So, it's actually very simple, you go back to that conversation about identity and loans, you will find that if you define cash as your enemy, you will be surprised who is the biggest contributor to cash.

Very early, after I became CEO, I looked at who generates cash in an economy and it's interesting that 35–40% of the world's circulating cash is generated by the government of a country in paying its citizenry. This could be paying a salary, pension, benefits or healthcare. So, the biggest administrator of cash is the government itself. The other sources of cash are all small and discrete: repatriation from your overseas relative, gifts from people, illegal transactions when you do not want to declare them. Those are all small in each individual one. They add up to 60%, but each of them is small, millions of things happening to millions of people. But government is one enormous chunk, and if you want to change something, you have got to intervene where there is scale.

So, we said let's go to where the governments are and see what their pain points are. They have two pain points. One, tax evasion, and the second is that there are several UN and IMF studies that show that 42% of the money that a government tries to deliver to its citizens never reaches them, in relief programs and benefits and so on. It gets taken along the way by middlemen with their sticky fingers. In the NGO world that's called 'leakage'. In our world, that is called 'theft', which is the problem.

When you think of the quantum of money being put out by governments and NGOs for humanitarian programs, if you think of 42% of that not reaching them – that is the lowest number. And I have learnt now through things we have done that that number is real. We introduced a phone-paid payment system for Afghanistan soldiers and police officers after the American military went in there a little while back. This was an effort to get them to not get the money through the warlords, but to get it directly from America into their phone. They all thought that their pay had gone up by 35%. They wrote letters saying, "Thank you for the pay increase of 35%." It was not a pay increase, it was our disintermediation of the sticky fingers' 35% by going directly and taking out the middleman, which was the Afghan warlords.

We saw this in case after case. We saw that in the World Food Programme (WFP) with the refugee crisis in Lebanon and Jordan and the refugee crisis in Greece. All the refugees were flooding into some islands of Greece, which I have actually inspected. In one of those islands, we started giving them ways to get their WFP contribution onto a card instead of giving them grain. As a result, the quantum of aid they received went up by 40%. All because of getting rid of the sticky fingers. Long story short, getting into that space of sticky fingers, which is where the governments' money goes, is where we went, and that's how financial inclusion was driven.

In actuality, lower amounts of cash and financial inclusion are completely intertwined, because cash is the friend of the person who has something to hide – because why do you hate taxes? Only if you've got taxes to evade. If you are relatively poor, you're living in a marginal economy, so there's nothing for you to hide. In fact, cash is then your worst enemy, because it forces you into the grey system and forces you away from access to cheap financing, insurance, things of that type that you and I take for granted. Thus, cash and financial inclusion are completely intertwined.

I was wondering how the Coronavirus has affected your vision and mission for a world beyond cash? – *Scholar, Megan Jones*

It's a tailwind because, funnily enough, while everybody was talking about going less cash and over the years there is an inexorable movement towards less cash in educated societies or in urban living, there are several global trends. Let me step back for a second. Urbanisation, globalisation, younger educated people, greater middle classes, more global travel, those are natural secular trends to reduce cash and increase electronic forms of payment. But the growth of the middle class in emerging economies, and the growth of prosperity in more markets actually grows faster. If you take the weighted average of developing economies, it grows faster than the growth in the developed world. Ironically, the percentage of transactions in cash changed little over the last decade.

So, in the United States, transactions in cash went from 70% to 40% today. But the problem is that in several other countries which are emerging into the world, they have gone up. Like India has gone up a great deal in terms of its ratio of contribution to personal consumption and transactions, but it's 95% cash. This shift works against you when trying to reduce cash as a percentage of transactions.

So, returning to your question, even in India during the Coronavirus crisis, the switch to digital is inexorable because there are no shops open, and even if the shops are open, people don't want to touch cash because they suddenly realise that cash is dirty. We used to put out studies on cash a long time ago – actually done by universities – which demonstrated that the average note, average dollar notes in the US, had traces of heroin on it forever; $1, $5, $10 notes, because that's what gets transacted in the drug trade. People used to laugh at it, and we would say, "This stuff is unhealthy." And they would say, "You've got to be kidding?" Jokes used to be cracked about how you are going to roll up a $100 bill and sniff it before you get enough, and that kind of muck was what was going on.

With the Coronavirus crisis, people feared it spread from surfaces, as compared to airborne diseases. They said cash is bad, and they went away from it, and that actually has been a huge tailwind. So, for example, contactless transactions for us globally were up 40% in the first quarter of 2020, and up another 40% in the second quarter. The overwhelming majority of them are for transactions under $20, which means they are replacing cash.

Australia was different right from the beginning. Four,

five years ago we launched contactless transactions in Australia. In five years, Australia went from zero contactless to 80% of transactions under $100. But you guys were unique – you are not the norm. The norm was outside – in the US, contactless was almost irrelevant and non-existent until the crisis. But Canada, Australia, Poland, Turkey, Hungary, the UK, they had more contactless transactions, while big markets like the US were very much stuck in the old form of payment. And contactless is both card as well as Apple Pay or Samsung Pay or whatever you prefer doing. So actually, the fight against cash has got a rocket booster coming out of Coronavirus.

> **I was wondering how do you see cybersecurity evolving in the future, and what role, if any, do you see artificial intelligence playing in that? –** ***Scholar, Amber Spurway***

Well, I think cyber is mission critical. You guys are digitally native as a generation, and we've learnt from you. I call myself digitally native today, but I picked it up because the young have driven it to all of us. If you believe in the power of 5G – irrespective of its competing standards – and where it's going, every device is going to become interconnected. Experts say there will be 50 billion connected devices by 2030. Today there are seven to eight billion already, and there are more adding up every month.

If your toaster, camera, car, shirt, glasses, watch and shoes will all be connected to the internet several of which already are, then every single device and every single interaction is a moment of truth where your privacy as a consumer, and therefore your safety and security, could be compromised by lack of attention to that topic.

Let us just talk about you and me and our personal data and our personal safety. When you're on your phone you signed up for a weather app and it actually took your contacts, why do the people making the weather app need your contacts to tell you what the weather is in Galapagos? They do not need that, but they will take it anyway. That is not even cybersecurity, it's just plain simple violation of privacy.

Then there's all the cyber angles to it, which are passwords. I mean, in America the most common password is 'password', and the second most common password is '0123456', and 70% of Americans have not changed their online banking account password from the date they opened their online banking account the first time, which on average is seven years ago. For instance, Andrew would be most likely guilty of what I'm just saying, because he's got 27 passwords to remember. These days he has to fly commercially, so he has to remember his American Airlines password, his Emirates Airlines password, his Costco password and his Australian Department of Motor Vehicles password, so what does he do? He changes his passwords; they're all Andrew1, Andrew1#, SAPaula – Paula is his wife's name – or something, all of which, by the way, a 10-year-old kid can crack in about seven minutes.

Passwords are really last century, and we make it really hard to remember them, and so we're only as strong as your weakest link. The weakest link right now in this interconnected world of 5G will be two links: (1) the individual consumer, and (2) the small business. For instance, when you go to your dentist, they make you fill out an entire form collecting everything you're allergic to and your social security number. If you think the dentist is keeping any of that information safe, you're sadly mistaken. Or if a child's school makes you fill out all your bank account information to debit for instant payment, do you think they're spending any money on cyber security? Forget about it, they're not.

So, I actually believe that this is a genuine issue that's alive today, and every one of us on this call has been hacked into. Every one of us. Some of us know it, some of us don't know it. And the only difference between those who know it and those who don't know it, is that the ones who know it, know it and are doing very little about it, and the ones who don't know it, don't know it and are therefore doing very little about it. That is the problem.

Unfortunately your generation doesn't seem to care about it. You are trading off convenience for security and privacy, and you do it consciously. You will leave your location services on your phone turned on all day long because you want to go to Google Maps and just check how to walk to the next block without having to say, "Put on location services." Well, throughout the day, your phone knows exactly where you went and how you walked and how far it took you and your pattern of movement. You may think it doesn't matter about you – but it matters.

I don't know how to explain this to people. You should be paranoid about your cybersecurity. You should be paranoid about your personal data. You should be paranoid about your safety, because it is your data, you have a right to monetise it for your benefit, not for somebody else's benefit. There is no reason to allow everybody else to make money out of your data. You should benefit from it individually and therefore protect it. You will only benefit from it if it's worth something, and it's only worth something if you protect it. These are just a handful of priorities for this coming generation.

I served on the Obama Commission (the Commission on Enhancing National Cybersecurity); I could give you 100 ideas of how we could make it better, but for example right now we are on a Zoom call, and I would question the exact safety and security of everything we're discussing. Especially if it were a conversation of great confidentiality. Similarly, this television we're speaking on, or the television you're on – if you're on a computer it's different – but if you're on a TV that has a camera, how do you as a consumer know whether that TV is safer in cyber terms than the other TV? There's no way for you to figure it out, unless you read every brief line in the fine print to figure out which one's safer.

I'm telling people we should invent the equivalent of a food nutrition label, which tells you you're getting X percentage of your fats by eating this cottage cheese compared to Y percentage by eating that. We need that guidance in simple terms for devices as well. So I as a layperson can know, this TV that cost me $1,000 is actually less safe than that TV that cost me $800. Those are the things I think we need to get into, and I think that's not a simple thing to do.

I was buying sneakers the other day, and the sneakers I bought are connected to the internet, as I learnt when I was buying them, and they transmit continuous data about my running patterns and where I'm running and I'm like, "Why do I need that?" All so that I can get an app download that tells me I ran 10,000 steps. If I know how many miles I ran, I can figure out how many steps that is. We just all need to be a little more thoughtful about convenience versus actual knowledge. I think that Facebook and Cambridge Analytica woke everybody else up to this, but we should have woken up to it before that. Facebook is the favourite punching bag right now, but this is not their fault alone. I think this is an endemic issue that needs fixing.

At the other end of the spectrum, what should governments and large corporations be doing to increase their cybersecurity? – Scholar, *James Orman*

That is the second part of this conversation. I think the first thing we all need to do is to realise the people who are trying to break into you are actually not individuals like you or me. While that happens, most of the big companies can spot and tackle those breaches. The real challenge is with organised crime and nation states. Australia's Prime Minister has recently publicly raised the issue of nation state attacks. Let me tell you, Australia knew about that some time ago.

It's not that your Prime Minister is the first one to know of it, he's just the first one to call it out. You should actually credit him for his toughness of mind to call it out. Therefore, you need to have a very deep public-private cooperation in this space, because not just a single company can handle this. Not Dow, not IBM, not JP Morgan, not Qantas, not Commonwealth Bank of Australia (CBA), not Sony, Toshiba, nor Mastercard. We cannot spend enough money by ourselves to provide all the cybersecurity the system needs, because the rogue players are spending many multiples of what we can, because of who they are. We need public-private cooperation at a completely new level, which includes information sharing.

To give you an example, today in the United States, if the Secret Service or the FBI come across chatter on the web that says that Mastercard is likely to be targeted by this syndicate or that country, they actually cannot come and tell me because they would be seen as benefitting a single corporation. What do they have to do? They have to issue public statements, like the payments industry may get targeted, the financial firms may get targeted. Well guess what, that's terrible, because it's one company that's getting targeted, but they're not allowed to say who.

We've got to change some basic rules of engagement as well. What I've been propagating is what I call a 'reverse Miranda'. The Miranda rights in the United States are when you get arrested, they tell you, "Hey, you have the right to remain silent, and anything you say could be used against you." You need the opposite of that in the case of cyber. If I know I'm getting attacked, I'm actually disincentivised at this moment in time to go to my regulator and proactively tell them, because if I do, when they come to examine me, they'll penalise me on my management rating. It happened to us at Citibank. You've got to give me the reverse Miranda, you've got to tell me, "Here, you can come and tell me what the problem is, I'll save you." But unfortunately today it is, "I got you, because you told me." That's nonsense. Some of these rules were created for the pre-digital era. But the problem is in the digital era, it's all about cross-border movement of data, commodity and trade, and that's a different trade agreement than we need. It doesn't fit the bill from what came earlier. In cyber, you need to have all these – you need that food nutrition label. You need to move from passwords to biometric security. You need to move to digital identities.

In Australia, we've launched a digital identity with universities, the government of Australia, a couple of banks and with Telstra, to identify that it's actually you who's going to sit for your exam and not somebody else whom you've paid to sit on your behalf, as that was happening in Australia in a few locations. Or if you were ordering liquor, and it was being delivered to your home today, in Australia, the delivery person who comes to deliver it to you has to take a photograph of your driving ID and actually send that to the head office. But if you do that on his phone, he now has your photograph, your full name, your exact date of birth, of course they know where you live, but also your driving licence number, or in some countries your national ID number. That is enough information to open a bank account with. That's dangerous, and you just gave it to get a bottle of booze delivered to your house. All the delivery person needed was to have somebody say you are above the age of 18.

To avoid this data leakage, what we are doing is collecting verification – not the raw information – from the driving licence agency, from the passport authority, from your bank where you opened an account. They have your birthdate, cross-check the three and say, "Oh, Megan is over

18 years old." Thus, the delivery company in the example just takes that information and moves on. You can do these things in a way to give you back your privacy, as compared to taking it away from you by giving you a distributed digital identity system. These are the things we've got to do. You don't do these alone, as this needs government help. In Australia what the government did to enable this is they made flat files of all government databases – driving licences, passport authority, all that data – and they allowed trusted parties to go in and query them, based on consumer permissions.

Scholar Reflection – Simeon Gover

Leadership truly is a fickle word. There exists the strong idea that there is no one definition of leadership, a phrase that I've come to understand more of the wisdom of by talking to different leaders. I was somewhat despondent upon realising how expansive the meaning of leadership was when Ajay Banga's comments about the 'decency quotient' resonated with me.

In essence, the decency quotient, or DQ, is a natural extension in growth from IQ, to EQ, to DQ. That is, to be successful early in life, you can rely on IQ. At a certain point, however, EQ becomes a necessity for further success. Finally, you reach another ceiling where EQ will only take you so far if you have not developed your DQ, your personal decency.

I was initially sceptical how being 'friendly' or 'kind' to everyone could lead to major business success until I realised DQ does not necessitate being nice or friendly to everyone. Rather, DQ is conducting decision-making in a fair and transparent manner. Ajay's words regarding the burden of difficult decision-making that comes with leadership were refreshing as they revealed some of the turbulence and uncertainty surrounding decision-making, further highlighting the need for a strong moral centre.

By strengthening your decency quotient, you can act in an intentionally fair and transparent way to both yourself and your colleagues. While empathy can be crucial, decency is now demanded in order to gain people's trust. Ajay's accentuation of decency in his career being essential highlighted to me the calling for leaders to act with decency in order to create change.

On ending this session, I reassessed my opinion of leadership. While leadership may be fickle, differing from one person to the next, I believe some fundamentals stay the same. One of these is the need for decency.

For my own career, and the careers of other emergent leaders, I think decency needs to be at the forefront of our minds. It is plainly irresponsible to assume anyone place trust in, or follow you, if you cannot show with transparency your inner morality and fairness. To resonate further, I think it's worth considering the absurdity of considering a leader without decency, one that operates under clear biases while behind closed doors, and ask yourself, "Would you follow them?"

4

Moving Beyond a Circular Economy to a Regenerative One

Paul Polman

14th July 2020
Currently, what we have is really a crisis of proportions that we have never had before. That we were not prepared for. Many people do not know how to deal with nor know how we will come out of it. Above all, what we are now debating depends on the leadership of people that will have a significant influence on our future direction. People are saying we need to go back to where we came from, or revert to the old world. But restarting the economy will not work. The old normal wasn't working either.

We were on the trajectory of climate change that is above three degrees warming by the end of the 21st century which is an absolute disaster for planet Earth. Even at our current rate, we're already losing 100 times more species than any historical patterns. We are destroying Mother Nature at a faster rate than it can replenish itself, and we are playing with planetary boundaries. Some people call it the sixth greatest extinction. One reason we have COVID-19 is, in fact, the result of expanding planetary boundaries, which causes these zoological diseases to come increasingly closer to humankind. We have had Zika, SARS, Ebola, and avian flu. Actually, they're increasing in frequency, as we destroy nature and as wildlife gets closer to human life.

COVID-19 itself should not be an actual surprise or a black swan. I think the black swan in all of this was the inability of governments around the world to work together. A lack of global cooperation and global governance that has really cost us dearly – not only in dealing with this crisis but also in the way we spent some of the money – and hopefully, we will learn to do better. It's good to remind ourselves of the financial crisis of 2008/2009 – which was of significantly lesser magnitude – as we didn't heed the warnings then. It was only a crisis initially of the financial market that became an economic, and afterwards, I would argue, a governmental crisis. But the way we got out of it, and the way we spent our money, wasn't actually very good. Little was spent on reorganising and restructuring our economies. Climate change and inequality continued to increase.

People were increasingly dissatisfied with the way politicians were handling things, and in many of the countries in the world, we saw populism and nationalism take over, and even xenophobia in some of these cases. At that time, many people felt banks were too big to fail, but people too small to matter. This has all resulted in the current crises. Which, next to a COVID-19 crisis, you would agree with me, is also an economic crisis, a financial crisis, and a crisis of governance. It has also become a social and inequity crisis, and last but not least, we've added to that a racial crisis. Now, because all these things are coming together, it might seem for some people to be overwhelming, but I think it's actually a good thing that they have come together. Not least because they're all related.

COVID-19 has exposed what we had difficulties getting through to the population at large: the relationship between biodiversity, climate change, human health, and inequality. Climate justice is one of the most important things that we need to work on. So thanks to COVID-19, perhaps more people are aware of this, and people realise that you cannot have healthy people on an unhealthy planet.

COVID-19 has also shown us that our social contract is broken. It's the people that we needed most during the height of the crisis that actually got paid the least. The healthcare workers, the truckers, the people that work in the food supply chain are often at the bottom of the chain, in subsistence. And it brought to light the gross inequalities, but also the fragility of our economic system. I've already said that the financial crisis was fairly predictable at that point in time, although it surprised some people. Any system where too many people feel they're not taking part, or that ultimately they're excluded from, these systems will rebel against themselves. That's why you already saw before the crisis, so many people going to the streets and making their voices heard. That's why we have seen extreme reactions in some of these political elections.

In the financial crisis, people took out one lesson, a

very simple lesson – *banks were too big to fail, but people were actually too small to matter.* And if we don't address this foremost in this crisis – that is, the human part of this – putting people at the centre, ensuring that it is going to be a more inclusive growth above anything else, then the recovery will not work. The biggest anxiety or angst that you now have with people is about their jobs, it's about the future. It's about the future of their kids. It's about an ability to include and be included. To have at least the dignity, respect, equity and equal opportunity that we should provide to each and everybody on this planet Earth.

Governments coming out of this crisis have already spent an estimated $16 trillion just to level the ship, to save lives and livelihoods. The International Monetary Fund (IMF) estimates that the global economy in 2020 will be down over 4%. I think by the end of the year, when the final tally is done, it would not surprise me if it's higher. Estimates suggest that about 370 million equivalent jobs have been lost because of this crisis, and obviously disproportionately affecting the young and women once more, who are in these fragile jobs that I've talked about.

We also see Oxfam estimating that COVID-19 will put another 500 million people back into poverty, and it's not surprising. If you talk to David Beasley, who runs the WFP, they're estimating that they need to provide emergency food now for 265 million people. That is more than double the rate that were on it before. The spending that we've done, the $16 trillion, just to put that in perspective, is over 100 times more than the money we spent during the Marshall Plan after the Second World War.

So the question now is, are we going to make the same mistake and be back in these Zoom classes in two, three, four, or five years? And yes, it's probably going to be sooner rather than later if we don't address some of these major issues. Or are we now waking up finally and becoming more responsible? The jury is out, and it requires the efforts of all of us to ensure that we build back better and that we come out better and stronger from this crisis.

So far, only 30% of the rescue money we put in has been spent on greening or more sustainable projects that would make us more resilient, and that would address some of these issues that we've been talking about. That's clearly not enough. In countries like the US, for example, you see the fossil fuel industry is getting a disproportionate amount of support. And it would not be smart of the governments of our world to put money into industries that frankly were already in decline before the crisis. Also, good to point out that there are still some major banks financing the coal expansions. Check your own bank.

This is a moment to put money into industries that actually are the industries of the future. These industries of the future are also those industries that create more and more resilient jobs. The investments that you need to create these jobs are significantly smaller than any other alternative. So here the governments have a choice: either spend a lot of money, be confused, inefficient and not create the jobs that are needed (i.e., the better-paying jobs, the more resilient jobs); or they can invest in future industries, R&D and education. This investment can be directed to retrofit our buildings to make them more eco-efficient, protect our natural environment and accelerate the move to green energy or electric vehicles. All of those things will create more jobs and a higher return for your money. The smart governments that do this, that understand this, are seeing the benefits from it, and now it's a question to get this awareness at scale across the world.

One of the more positive things that has happened in the last few weeks is not only that citizens of this world are speaking up, but 95% of the citizens in any country in the world don't want to go back to where they came from. Employees are speaking up, equally importantly, we're seeing walk-outs from employees in many of the big companies, if their CEOs don't take drastic action on climate change, or if they don't fulfil a better part of that social contract, and many other things. The financial market is getting interested as well. We now have the Task Force on Climate-Related Financial Disclosures (TCFD), which has already over $109 trillion of assets under management, calling for disclosure on climate-related risks, a price on carbon and for decarbonisation plans.

Unsurprisingly, the financial markets are moving, because during this crisis, companies that were operating more under an environmental, social and governance (ESG) model tended to have a better return. I think that balance has shifted to the more responsible side of the equation, away from the militant treatment and shareholder primacy obsession that we've lived with over the last few decades. So you see companies moving in great numbers actually, over 80% of the CEOs want to come out better – and I don't understand the last 20%, I need to meet them still. We have now 25% of the economy, over 1,100 of the biggest companies taking climate action. Despite the COVID-19 crisis, they are accelerating their climate action. We are also seeing governments starting to move: 75% have now set net zero commitments for 2050/2060 (China) versus 25% before the crisis. That is actually one of the more encouraging things. Because if governments don't move, I don't think we'll get to these objectives that we've set ourselves.

The main catalyser for change right now is probably Europe with their Green Deal, the biodiversity packages, their farm to fork policy, where they've clearly set net zero targets for climate by 2050. These policies are now being echoed in other bodies around the world. Europe will use its scale and its size to see how it can not only decarbonise, but become a leader in green technology for the world. Europe can use its size and skill to influence other parts of the world. A good example of that is the current Mercosur responsible sourcing deal that is being worked with Latin America, where a high emphasis is being put on not taking supply that is linked to deforestation.

We see other governments starting to move. The government of Japan, which has been trailing in the past, has decided to close 100 coal plants between now and 2030. That is a big move from where we were even a few weeks ago. The government of France, as I'm sitting here, is closing 30 coal plants. We can see that clear shift happening in other countries as well. In countries like Canada, for example, some others have made bailout subsidies contingent towards greening these different business models.

So I think the movement is starting and is picking up speed. If we can speed that up to about 30% to 40% of the global economy, I think we'll get close to a tipping point. A tipping point that is needed for humanity. There, frankly, is no alternative. A tipping point that is absolutely beneficial for business, but not every business will benefit. All businesses will obviously have to adjust and change, and if they don't, then they'll go to the graveyard of dinosaurs. But new businesses will develop, and the economy will be so much better for it. A good indicator that the market is appreciating that fact is the market value of Tesla, which is now the biggest market value of any car company in the world. I think it passed Toyota just last week alone, and I think that will continue.

Whilst it is not clear in all aspects of what the future looks like, there are still many uncertainties. There is no question it will be a future where governments play a bigger role, because they've invested so much money. Some of that has to be translated into equity shares in companies, for example.

We also will see a bigger role of technology. Satya Nadella, who heads Microsoft, was saying it clearly that in the last two or three months, we have done more than what we expected in the coming five years. And he's probably right on that. So technology will change a lot of things. And also for the better, I hope. Notwithstanding the digital challenges we face, for example, with Facebook and others.

Finally, I think there will be a period ahead of us where global governance will be difficult. I don't want to deny that, nor do I want to be optimistic. I can give you a story of happiness, and obviously the US elections in November are going to play a big role in that. But broadly, our global governance and the functioning of our global institutions need a drastic overhaul, and that will take time. So in the absence of being able to depend on that global governance, my simple philosophy has always been that we cannot sit still and cannot sit at the sidelines and blame the politicians.

We obviously can change our political systems, and I encourage you to look at that in any country where you have that opportunity to do so. I was very glad to see that 40% of your students at the University of Queensland are actually foreign students as well. So you have a brilliant mix at your university. Always use your right to vote and be part of this political process, it's very important. But I think above all, in the next 10 years, it's going to be the private sector who has the resources, the funding, the technology and many more things to de-risk the political process and drive change.

We saw the initial signs of that with the Paris Agreement and climate change. We're now seeing that in areas of social justice – the lesbian, gay, bisexual, and transgender (LGBT) community and others are good examples of that – where private sectors have forced governments to move faster. Now we are seeing this around the areas of biodiversity and a broader discussion around the green recovery. So that is where we are.

What we now need is to focus on creating that scale of impact. It's clear that many companies want to move in a better direction, but there are some constraints that make it difficult for individual companies to achieve all these objectives. So what we are focussed on now with IMAGINE and with some other efforts, is to bring a collective of companies together across a value chain – trying to get to about 25% to 30% of a total value chain at CEO level and drive these tipping points. When we do this, we see an accelerated change for the better.

There are two clear guiding principles which will not change. First is the Paris Agreement, which clearly calls for a net zero by 2050 – Andrew Liveris and I are both co-chairs of the B20[3] Energy, Sustainability and Climate Taskforce, which has made strong recommendations to all the G20 countries. The second guiding principle for us is the 17 Sustainable Development Goals (SDGs). These famous 17 goals that were approved in September 2015 by 193 countries in the United Nations. It was a simple goal to eradicate poverty irreversibly and do that in a more sustainable and equitable way, with the simple goal of not leaving anybody behind. That is how I began my short talk, and how I wish to end it. So with that, I'm happy to open it up to questions.

You talked a little about the system of global governments being broken, so how do you think it should be updated if governments can't do it alone anymore? – *Scholar, James Orman*

Well, there are many things that obviously need to be done. The first driver is citizen's power, which is very important. Because when citizens speak up, governments tend to move, because they are sensitive to their voices and don't underestimate the voices of the young. Also, getting fair representation tends to do better.

3 The B20 represents the global business community across G20 member states.

If you look at the countries like New Zealand, Iceland, Norway, Denmark, Finland, and Taiwan, that have done better during this COVID-19 crisis, these are countries that are actually led by women. I don't think that's a coincidence. Because it needs a certain leadership style of cooperation, of empathy, of listening, of morality, of partnership, of purpose that seems to be driven more right now by the female gender than the male. So exercising your voting rights and ensuring that we have gender diversity are very important preconditions.

The second driver is the financial markets. The reality is, whether we like it or not, if the financial markets don't move and don't see the benefits, it's very difficult to get the whole economic system to move at scale. To make this move, two of the institutions that are very important, the IMF and the World Bank, these institutions are working with all the ministers of finance, the ministers of the central banks, and there we are starting to see climate change moving higher on the agenda. The situation will probably be better after November in the US, depending on the election outcome, because we really need that stewardship from America still, whether we like it or not. We need to look at the multilateral development banks and these two great institutions, to see if we can bring climate change higher on the agenda. This includes climate finance with debt restructuring for the emerging markets and related policy changes.

The third driver is what I briefly talked about, that is the private sector. We need to get enough critical mass of the private sector to move. I think that is going to be probably easier than the second driver I talked about. But both need to be in sync, otherwise you are being held back. The private sector needs to speak up and de-risk the political process. Take, for example, removal of preferred subsidies, the world still has $500 billion of preferred subsidies on fossil fuels. We also need green infrastructure, but many of the laws and regulations actually undermine this objective. We must speak up and ensure governments that reforms are okay. Likewise for additional spending. We have to help governments get confidence to spend it on greening the economies. We also need the financial industry to get involved in longer-term financing. So changes need to occur at the individual level, the financial level, and at the private sector level.

> ***IMAGINE*** **has been involved with some really incredible work. I was particularly interested in its role in the Fashion Pact, and I'd like to ask, what do you believe is the most difficult aspect of bringing together these really influential and high-powered individuals, and what do you believe this can teach us about leadership? –** ***Scholar, Javan McGuckin***

That's an excellent question. So the premise of IMAGINE is very simple. We've all been CEOs and one thing that we all discovered as CEOs is that even with leading companies like Dow or Unilever, you can only do so much yourself. Ultimately, you need some of these frameworks that we talked about, or governments, to put the right structures in place, to not have the free riders around you. You also need your other competitors to change in some areas as well. And frankly, sometimes you simply don't have the scale to drive change yourself. For example, in our industry, in consumer goods, you produce a lot of plastic if you like it or not. We don't want plastic in the oceans, we all agree on that. But it's very difficult for each individual company to solve that. Even a company like Unilever can't put recycling units in every place that we operate. That is a task that needs to be done in partnership.

IMAGINE is a for-benefit corporation focused on accelerating the implementation of the SDGs focused especially on climate change and inequality. The theory of change is to put a critical mass of CEOs together by industry sector and across the value chain to drive towards tipping points. We estimate we need about 25–30% of a sector together to achieve this. We then focus on human change, making us collectively more courageous, and systems change. Industries we are currently looking at are food, fashion, tourism, and finance. All having a big impact on the SDGs.

For example, fashion is actually the second most polluting industry in the world. People might not know that, but the bulk of plastic in the oceans, 46% according to some studies, is actually from fashion. It's the microfibres in your clothes and the washing. They're the most dangerous ones, because they enter the food chain quickly. It's not the plastic bottles that you see that get the attention, because obviously what you see is more emotional. It's also an industry that destroys biodiversity. Cotton as a crop is very harmful to biodiversity, and entire regions in the world have been turned into deserts because of it. For example, regions like Kazakhstan or Mongolia, where you have had totally unsustainable practices. Additionally, there are the poor labour standards which is apparent to everyone as a significant issue. The industry is known for incredible waste.

Consequently, we attacked the fashion industry and looked at three areas: *climate change, regenerative cotton,* and *single-use plastics.* One of our conditions is that anybody that takes part has to sign up to be net zero by 2050. The other two areas relate to biodiversity, on getting to regenerative cotton and on plastics, getting out of single-use plastics. When we launched IMAGINE we started with 30 companies about a year ago. These were the more progressive companies and now we are at 68 companies which represent about 30% to 35% of the total industry. So we are at the tipping point.

What we see is not surprising, that if these 30 CEOs are together, they become more courageous because they listen to each other. They are obviously leading CEOs, but there is a bit of a positive competition on the race to the top. Then other companies want to join as well. We have 68 now, because nobody wants to lose out – the fear of missing out. This makes other companies want to be part of this movement. We call it the courageous collective.

When you have critical mass, civil society like NGOs or governments want to work with you, not against you. We then get these partnerships that are ultimately needed to drive these broader changes. For example, in one of my roles, I advise the French Government. President Macron and the French Government have put some quite good legislation in place against waste in the fashion industry. Often we get the wrong legislation because governments are short term focussed, but if you get the right legislation, it also means you are dealing with the underlying causes. The added benefit is that you actually have less legislation. So these are all good things.

The crucial factor is getting stakeholders in the industry together. The entire way we've set up our private sector is around a win/lose dichotomy – if I do something, it has to be to my advantage, and it has to be to your disadvantage. It's a secret what I do and I should keep it to myself. However, what we're saying here is, the price for humanity is much higher than for your individual gain. It's a bit of the prisoner's dilemma. If we all don't do it together, we all go under. And this is really what we're talking about now, especially when it gets to planetary boundaries.

For example, take a company like Olam in agriculture. Olam has done excellent work with the small hold farmers, who are very poor. Most of the poor farmers in the world are mono-crop smaller growers. They are often constrained and use slave labour, or child labour, or a combination of these. To counter these issues, Olam have developed an excellent system with two million farmers. They have made it open, because they think it's so important to build that social inclusion, unlike other players in the agricultural industry. Olam's system integrates traceability and disintermediation of people in the supply chain who take a margin which keep the farmers poor. In this way, we can create this cumulative race to implement the SDGs.

The most difficult thing for the CEOs right now is the global governance situation. In most countries, CEOs are more ambitious themselves than the speed that the government is moving. In the short-term, it's not surprising, because we have to deal with a crisis we've never dealt with before. But increasingly we need to get these governments to not hold us back. The gap between the private sector ambition of that group of CEOs and where the governments are is simply becoming too big. And if you run too far ahead, then you actually risk even doing more damage than good. From a business point of view, we need to be sure that we put people at the centre. In all of this, it should be about inclusion, livelihoods and the new social contract. For a lot of CEOs, that is still a challenge.

Many CEOs understand the *environmental* part of ESG, but more difficult for them is still the S part. The *social* part also has to do with paying fair taxes, which also has to do with providing safety nets around people, which also has to do with getting out of COVID-19 and taking responsibility for your value chain. Many companies are in a corporate social responsibility mode, everything that's under their control, they will make commitments on. But when it gets to your total impact, they are a little more hesitant. Many companies still think that you can outsource your value chain, and also outsource your responsibility. That doesn't work anymore. So we need to get the CEOs to that higher level, especially on the social part. We need to be in sync with the governments.

Andrew (Liveris) created an excellent model on handprint, footprint and blueprint, which has become a guiding model for many companies. For instance, Andrew suggests that what blueprint really means is if I'm a company like Dow and I run the company, sure I have environmental effects, and sure I need to produce things, and sure I need chemicals, but I still need to look at my total impact. Look at all the material I produce to ensure that food doesn't get wasted. Look at the houses I insulate, so that we don't lose 80% of our energy without having had the benefit from it, and so on. Companies need to look at their total impact, including all the people in this case.

The biggest challenge is leadership. We know what we have to do. There are many CEOs that might not want to say it publicly, but you talk with everybody privately. Nobody wants more unemployment; nobody wants more air pollution; nobody wants more people going to bed hungry. Yet collectively, this is the direction we're driving. But most CEOs know what they want to do, and they're good people. It takes a bit of courage, because if you want to drive these changes – it's not difficult. You need to decarbonise an economy, you need to move to a circular, regenerative economy, you need to move the financial markets to the longer-term, and you need to get a more inclusive growth model.

These changes must be done when governance isn't working, which is a bigger challenge than any of us have ever faced. So it takes courage, and courage comes as much from the French word 'couer', from the heart, as it comes from the brain. On that road of change, you have a lot of sceptics and cynics around that want to attack you. To tell you that it cannot be done or there is a vested order who wants to protect itself. It's not so easy, and it requires really a strong moral compass and a powerful level of leadership. So how do we create more leaders?

The Liveris Academy is important to create these courageous leaders of the future. Over 50% of the world's population is below 30, and yet they are grossly excluded. As I have advocated, the youth should get a seat at the table. Especially now that governments are spending $10 trillion again, to get us out of the mess that they knew was coming. There's nothing surprising here, only the magnitude of it. But they spent $10 trillion, and that's only the initial stabilisation process. All this debt that comes on the shoulders of the next generation. So if we are borrowing from the youth, should we not ask them, how should we come out of this? The vast majority of young people – 97% in a recent Ipsos poll – say we want a greener, more inclusive economy, and if you don't create it, we'll vote you out of office. So my suggestion to you is, you know who they are, so vote them out of office if they don't create it.

In what ways did your experience of the tragedy in the Mumbai hotel[4] change how you led as a CEO and as a businessperson? – *Scholar, Victoria Barnes*

So let me take it in a broader context, because I don't like to talk about it too much. I think leadership is being formed by what happens to you throughout your life, and it's the tougher things, if you look at where we learnt most in our businesses as CEOs on a very left-brain level, was from

4 A series of coordinated terrorist attacks were carried out in Mumbai over four days in November 2008, drawing global condemnation. At least 174 people were killed, and more than 300 injured. Paul Polman, then CEO-elect of Unilever, was attending a business dinner in Mumbai's Taj Mahal Palace Hotel at the time it was attacked.

the mistakes we made. I have always said I became CEO because I probably made more mistakes than anybody else. And people may laugh, but it actually is true. The things that I remember are things that I would have done differently. It's the mistakes that you remember, because obviously you don't want to repeat them. These are the things that make you a great leader.

Leadership is to understand your weaknesses and to learn from the things that you've done wrong. Sometimes it is as an individual and sometimes it is as a business. Your character gets formed by a lot of things in life and these are crucibles that we all have, and they will continue until the moment you pass on from this wonderful planet. These crucibles will form you, who you are, and how you think about things. Some of that might be a spiritual component, in which environment you grew up in.

I grew up just after the Second World War, where my parents were deprived of university. I don't know if they could have gone or not, but my father was 15 when the war started and 20 when the war was finished. So he couldn't go to high school in the Netherlands. The same was true for my mother. So, their goal was to get their six children educated and to university. My father had two jobs, worked in a factory, to make sure that we could have a bar of soap to give us hygiene, and food in our bellies. They did what they could so that we could take part in all the other activities that helped us develop into who we are. They were unselfishly putting themselves to the service of others, knowing that by doing so, they were better off themselves as well. My parents also actively advocated for peace, having seen the devastating effects of the war. It is this service of others, which is why this great European experiment is actually a grand experiment. It's the longest period in Europe, with no wars or conflicts that we should really be mindful of. Many things shape us. For instance, you might have a death in your family that forms you.

Another example of experience shaping people, I observed when I worked in Newcastle. There I saw, for the first time, second generation people being unemployed. Girls of 13, 14 years old that, the only procession they could have is a baby, so they became pregnant, making their situations worse. This inspired me to get involved in some community building activities. Another experience that shaped me was my friend who was blind. We climbed Mount Kilimanjaro with eight blind people. That was the start of my blind foundation, the Kilimanjaro Blind Trust Africa, which now has 26,000 blind children in schools in East Africa, that I run with my wife.

So these are all the experiences that make you realise who you are, who you are not, who you should be, and who the genuine people in society are, whom you should serve. You become a genuine leader the moment that you discover it's not about yourself. When you can truly put yourself to the service of others. That requires, undoubtedly, some financial security to look after your own circle. Most important is to be at the sweet spot of what the world needs, what you enjoy and what you are good at.

To me, leadership is first and foremost being a good human being. We always quote the Ghandis or the Dr Martin Luther Kings or the Nelson Mandelas, and they were incredible people, but change happens at all levels. Think about all these doctors that started treating us for Ebola or COVID-19. You know, 20% of the medical community actually lost their lives because they were infected early on, not knowing what they were treating. The same was happening with Ebola. So these are the heroes. Or the teachers that, for a pittance of a salary, teach the blind or the deaf-blind. Come with me once to Kilimanjaro and you'll see how they dedicate themselves 24 hours to give someone else their dignity. These are the actual heroes.

In Mumbai, I saw the same acts of service. It was not something that you want to repeat, but you see that there is a lot of goodness. That evil needs to be fought with goodness, and at the end of the day, goodness prevails. There were more babies born that night in Mumbai than people lost their lives. There were more people helping us when we got out of that terrible ordeal that showed that goodness, and we all became a little bit more Indian. We all became a little bit more citizens of this world as well.

We know that at the root of all this terrorism and violence, which masquerades often as religion, is often poverty and exclusion. So all the more reason for us to ensure that we get inclusive economic growth. It is actually very sad to me that to implement the SDGs would require approximately $3 trillion a year over 15 years. That would do the job. Right now we have spent $16 trillion on COVID-19, because we didn't do the job. The cost of climate change is $5.3 trillion. Think of the recent floods in Japan and in China where hundreds of people lost their lives. The world spends 8% of its $90 trillion global economy on conflict prevention and wars. That is nearly three times more than what it would take us to implement the SDGs. So here we are spending all this money to deal with the symptoms, whilst it is much cheaper to deal with the underlying cause. This has always been my argument, but we have waited so long that the argument is even more compelling now. Therefore, the financial markets have moved to ESG and push it now, because they finally discovered this.

When people say my fiduciary duty is to maximise shareholder return, then considering where we are in this world, they must actively support ESG. Because if they don't support ESG, they now undermine the long-term profitability of the shareholders. We've shifted the balance from treating the symptoms to treating the cause. We are now at this point that we just need to systemise it to get all the different stakeholders aligned and understanding that. For instance, every dollar we spend on solving air pollution, we get a $30 economic benefit. Every dollar we spend on nutrition to avoid malnutrition, we get a $16 benefit. By giving women the same land rights, finance, education, access as we do men, we unlock the global economy by $25 trillion. For every SDG you look at, there's a payout that is 10 to 15 times higher.

Here is the secret: there are tremendous financial returns in implementing the SDGs. I was fortunate enough to work with the former United Nations Secretary General Ban Ki-moon to be the business representative in developing the SDGs, which gave me great insights into them. I then implemented that into Unilever, and the organisation just became so much stronger. We had a 300% shareholder return. We had a 19% return on invested capital, despite doing 67 acquisitions. We outgrew our industry by two times. That's why it was so ridiculous when again someone came in, a corporate raider who wanted to play the financial game.

As a result of financial success by doing the right things, Unilever wasn't leveraged, which was important. During COVID-19, Unilever was the first company that provided $500 million in credit to its supply chain, whilst banks were still too careful to lend. Because the banks will never want to do anything that has a risk attached, unless you and I take the risk, or the government carries the risk. Unilever and similar companies can do that, because we're running these companies responsibly for the longer term.

Focusing on society as we did at Unilever is what corporate citizenship looks like. I get so many questions from companies about: What does good corporate citizenship look like? What is this future of moral or human or societal capitalism? We need to make companies understand that they now need to be part of a bigger movement than themselves. Just like people need to be part of a bigger thing than themselves, which makes you grow. The same concept is true for companies. In the future, if companies cannot show that they have a positive impact on society and look beyond their own self-interest, I don't think they will exist anymore.

This societal shift is already happening – when I was born, the average lifetime of a publicly traded US company was 67 years. Now, it's 17 years. The average lifetime of a CEO was 17 years then, now the average lifetime of a CEO has dropped to below five years. So we don't know how to run companies, nor do we have the right leaders to run it in the current environment. This is a wonderful opportunity for the youth today. I'd like to be born now, as you have more opportunities than ever. You have a longer life than ever. You have more access to technology and other things than any of us had. There are more ideas out there than we know how to deal with. I mean, this is the land of opportunity. So it's actually the best time to get this new level of leadership that you all represent.

Overhauling the sustainability of large companies like Unilever isn't something that many companies have achieved. And you've outlined how successful that was for the stock price and the value of your company. So what was it about your leadership in particular that enabled such a significant change? – *Scholar, Flynn Pearman*

I don't know if it has been successful, but that is what we are still aiming for. I've said already, if Unilever did all these things and share price shoots up, but other companies don't follow, I still can't look my kids in the eye. We haven't solved the problem. At the moment, we have COVID-19 to contend with, so let's be realistic: there's not much to celebrate yet. Perhaps my views are shaped by my Calvinistic upbringing in the Netherlands.

One area of regret for me, and I was attacked fair and square for quite a long time on, was because I didn't provide enough facts and data, or do a good enough job to explain the benefits of SDGs to the financial community or other stakeholders. I also regret that we weren't more aggressive, and should have moved faster on some things at Unilever, as it became a company, that probably was less bad, but not yet to that ultimate level five that I talk about. So there's a lot to be done.

I also think that success is not necessarily the share price. We experienced a 300% increase in share price at Unilever over that 10-year time period. However, at that time, the interest rates were basically zero and half the world was on negative interest rates, so investing in stocks was the obvious choice for money managers. So is that a measure of success? Someone compared us to Kraft Heinz. The latter focuses on a few billionaires, who then earn more billions, whilst we focus on the billions of people. I'd rather be a billionaire, focussing on the billions of people, than a few billionaires. So in Unilever, we could do this, perhaps because first, there are fantastic people.

When I came into Unilever 10 years ago or 12 years ago, it wasn't in the best shape. But there was an enormous opportunity. One of my previous bosses told me once, the best job you can get in your life is a job that has a low base and a lot of reserves. What I found in Unilever was a low base and a lot of reserves. I could find a lot of efficiencies to get the money to invest in the business to make it grow, and I could find a lot of things that were easy fixes to bring common sense back to our strategies and make the business successful. So then we hired a lot of good people and brought a lot of good people into the right jobs. I had to change 70 of the top 100 people in the first year, more or less, to be aligned with this new strategy. The strategy made the company run, and we should not forget that. We talk a lot about sustainability, but at the end of the day, you need to have the right price and you have to have the right quality. Your products need to be in the right place, you need to be sure that the basics of how you run the business work, as much as the reason for how you run the business.

This gets me to the next point, which is the purpose. When we came to the stronger purpose of wanting to decouple our growth from environmental impact and increasing our overall social impact, which we did very early, it was very appealing. It was very appealing to the young people in our company, but surprisingly it was very appealing throughout, because it gave a bigger sense of belonging, a bigger sense of meaning. We did two things that I think in hindsight were smart, but I didn't know it at that time. We said we don't have all the answers, and we can't do it alone, which made us human. It created enormous partnerships with others, some partnerships were with big organisations like the United Nations Children's Fund (UNICEF) or the WFP, others were with non government organisations (NGOs) like Save the Children, Oxfam, Greenpeace, or the World Wide Fund for Nature (WWF). We put 50 targets out there, and people said, "Why do you put 50 targets out there? They're only going to attack you or you won't be there in 10 years anyway to be held accountable for that." It turned out that I was there 10 years later.

If you don't put your targets out there, you don't get that transparency that is needed to build trust. You know, transparency is the basis for trust, which is the basis for prosperity. So that plan actually turned out to be energising, also, because it was more holistic. Initially, we leaned towards the environmental side, but changed quickly with the Rana Plaza collapse in Bangladesh, which killed at least 1,132 people (mostly women) and injured more than 2,500. By the way, they were paid 26 cents an hour, as close as you can get to modern-day slavery. As a result, we also said we need to put that social component much higher. Thus, we brought in the best people we could find from the textile industry. After which, we put in social targets like creating jobs for five million small hold farmers, two million women, and all the other things. That made the model more robust, and our partnerships made the model more resilient.

At the end of the day, it might surprise you, but as a CEO, we don't know much. In fact, the CEO knows the least about the company. The finance director knows more about finance, that's why you make him finance director. Otherwise, you should be the finance director. The marketing director knows more about marketing. The person who runs Brazil for you knows more about Brazil. The person who runs the Dove brand or the Lipton brand knows more about those brands. Obviously, we are all experts in Ben & Jerry's – that goes as a given. But most people, if not all people, know more than you do. So your job is to make them successful. Basically, your job is to share their stories, give them the credit, aggregate the bigger picture, open doors, move boundaries; so they can grow in there and they will.

If you take care of people, then over and over again, you will see that people will take care of you. The best way for you to grow and develop is to grow others and develop others. That is really what we were doing in an integrated way, with this Unilever Sustainable Living Plan, which I wouldn't say was all success. We also had some lessons there which we can talk about another time, but there were things I would do differently now. More broadly, I think that's the direction you want companies to go in, that should be the minimum standard today. I'm already thinking about what should be the next one or two things. I talked about the social part, so I won't repeat myself, but that has to have a whole different dimension.

We were the only company that issued a human rights report twice. I hope my successor, who is very good, is now working on the third one. We haven't seen many other companies do that. So the social part is an important part. The second one is companies need to think in regenerative terms. You cannot think in circular anymore, you must think in regenerative, as we have overshot the planetary boundaries. Johan Rockström with the Resilience Institute has shown that as a planet, we need to restore and repair. That's regenerative. So business models need to be net positive, they cannot be neutral anymore.

Many people think if I'm not bad, I'm good. No, if you are not bad, you are not bad, but you're not good. You're only good if you do good, not if you do no bad. So we need to get these business models to net positive, but that's a whole new topic for another time.

Considering the world that capitalism has given us, which isn't great, do you think it is compatible with sustainability, or do we have to build something

better and adopt a different economic framework, like donut economics? – *Scholar, Megan Jones*

It all depends on how you define it. After the Great Depression, Franklin Roosevelt in the US bent the growth of capitalism with the New Deal. He introduced social security, healthcare and several other things and made America function. In the last 30 years, we've lifted more people out of poverty than at any time in human history. It's not only China, it's in many parts of the world.

Capitalism in that sense has been a tremendous creator of wealth but it's also clear that if you don't evolve systems, then it's like these multilateral institutions. Most of them were started in the days of the Bretton Woods system in 1944 – they haven't been adjusted and that's why we have a problem with global governance now in a company – if you started in 1944.

We started well before then but we have had strategy adjustments 10, 15, 20, 30 times. So the same is true with capitalism, I don't really care about the word, but we do need to evolve it.

In 1934, when Simon Kuznets invented gross domestic product (GDP) he said, "That's a measure of industrial output, but don't use it as a measure of economic success." That is because GDP doesn't measure negative externalities and it doesn't measure a lot of positive externalities. GDP goes up if we make war, but not when we make peace. GDP also goes up if we have a lot of pollution and burn a lot of coal, but clean air will not be in the GDP. So GDP doesn't measure the externalities and it doesn't measure income inequality either, there's an overall measure, but not a measure of distribution. So there are a lot of fallacies in GDP and many people are looking for alterantives.

The famous Bhutan Gross National Happiness (GNH) started that debate. That obviously is too small a concept to change the world but I think people are now looking for alternatives. Europe is now looking with the Green Deal, to better define outcomes. So we have to evolve this capitalism to make it more inclusive and to make it more sustainable. I think people are starting to understand that then capitalism is okay.

The fundamental requirement is that we must measure what we treasure. If we don't put a price on carbon, for example, then we will not achieve carbon neutrality quickly. By the way, 20% of the world now has a price on carbon or a cap-and-trade system and their economies are doing fine, they're actually stronger now. In total, the data are increasingly overwhelming but you need to put a price on those externalities, so that is one important thing that needs to be done.

I think we need to change our tax system to tax capital, which is currently not taxed. That's why rich people become richer, and we've all benefited from that. But we need to 'untax' labour and tax capital. That is because the current system was designed when we had no shortage of materials, but a shortage of labour. So we need to change the economic system. We need to change our measurement system. Capitalism, or whatever we would call it, would be fine if we change the definition of growth.

Ultimately, growth is not making more stuff as there's

only so much you can dig out of the Earth and dump in factories and then use it and put it in the oceans. With our current trajectory, there will be more plastic in the ocean than fish by 2050. So we need to define growth in different ways. In overall wellbeing, the quality of education, the quality of air, the peace that we have, the ability to not only reuse chemicals or materials, but actually upscale them, and provide the economic systems and incentives to do that.

There's no conflict with lifting people out of poverty if you think about it that way. A good example of that is music. When Andrew Liveris and I were born – which is the time of when your grandfathers were born, probably – we had these long playing records, these big records. You might still see them in the stores now and then, but then it became a compat disc (CD). I remember thinking at the time, that is the end of how you can do it, CDs cannot be beaten. However, now we have Spotify and the energy that runs it is green. So now we have unlimited music with green energy at a price that is zero. It makes us happier and it doesn't have to cost the Earth – that is the way I think we need to think about many other things. That just cuts to the heart of this regenerative system, which provides us with tremendous opportunities.

Just in Europe, the circular economy alone has unlocked $1 trillion; that's why Europe is so keen to lead with the circular economy package. Countries that don't understand that are regions that will be at a disadvantage. If you think about it that way, and design your policies around it that way, you can have a higher level of wellbeing for more people. So my simple answer is yes, at the end of the day, leave capitalism as a word, but make it work by making those changes that we talked about.

Scholar Reflection – Lilly Van Gilst

When listening to Paul Polman speak, one imperative is resounding: leaders of the 21st century must do well by doing good. Gone are the days where anything is a means to an end of profit. Companies have a responsibility, encoded in a social licence to operate, to evaluate their net impact and make sure it is positive. They cannot hide by outsourcing value chains and responsibilities with issues such as climate change and global inequality.

In the past, I have perceived a dichotomy between being profitable in business and doing what is right by people and the environment. However, Paul's ideas and methods provide a crucial reframing, showing that not only is doing good things possible as a business leader, it is the fundamental tenet upon which to act. Leaders must embed the core of their morals and values for a better world, rather than trying to reconcile the detriments they are impacting. It is a courageous task and it requires change. He has done it himself at Unilever, but Paul doesn't elude that making necessary changes are easy. They bring about sceptics and cynics, who will challenge your vision as a leader. This requires inner determination, but even more so, it requires collaboration.

One person, no matter how good a leader, cannot solve global issues alone. There is a balance to tip, a sort of precipice beyond which momentum will gather itself. Paul shows how the positive race to the top relies not on your usual competition against, but rather your collaboration with. Consequently, building genuine connections with like-minded peers is a crucial skill for leaders of the 21st century. In listening to Paul Polman and Andrew Liveris interact, it is so evident the mutual respect, admiration and accountability shared between the two. They serve as an exemplar of the good things that happen when people who work hard, listen, foster equality and champion sustainability collaborate.

It can be done. It must be done.

5

The Ethics of Leadership and the Impacts of Decision-Making

Ginni Rometty

15th July 2020

Business leaders at all levels, in any industry, have an obligation to model responsible stewardship. At IBM, that means building trusted relationships among all of our constituents, preparing society for innovations, and committing to diversity and inclusion in both business and society. These are not just moral decisions. They are business decisions, necessary to meet the expectations of our clients, investors, and employees. In other words, corporate strategy and corporate responsibility are not mutually exclusive. This is the ethical framework I have used to guide my decision-making throughout my career.

Previously, you said that it is important to stand for policies and positions rather than for politics. Are

these not intrinsically all linked? How do you work to distinguish between these and communicate your key standings and values to your colleagues, within the constraints of a company hierarchy? – ***Scholar, Lilly Van Gilst***

First, I can remember why I had to quote that phrase, policies versus politics, and it probably had never really come to the forefront until this last presidential election, when I had many employees who had views on both sides. At the time, it was very polarising, and people felt we shouldn't be involved in anything. On each side, people felt that way. I really went back to our archives and looked, and the leader of IBM had been involved with every president of the United States since Woodrow Wilson. I myself had been with almost every leader of every country in this world that was of any significance. It was, to me, a really powerful lesson to people, to say I am all about policy, and it is not about the politics, meaning the personality or the moment or the party.

In fact, it's a wonderful lesson for life actually, irrespective of which political party is in there, you fight for what you believe based on your values. Not long ago, IBM announced an American work policy committee (the American Workforce Policy Advisory Board) that was put together by the former Secretary of Commerce and Ivanka Trump. It's about bringing people from underserved communities into a new form of education. Not necessarily a four-year degree to start, but give them actual access to opportunity.

The reason I bring this up is someone said to me, "Hey

look, the environment is too political right now with an election going on. We shouldn't do this." I said, "No, I'm going to go ahead and do the announcement. This has always been our position. We have stood for education and access to opportunity. I don't care about what's happening around us." That to me is a very principled decision and we went ahead. There will be some minority voice who, perhaps, gets a loud voice because of social media, but that doesn't matter.

My view is that if you stick to what you believe on a topic, you will always be on the right side of history. With my team, I think that's a really easy thing to say here. Are there things that are important to us and when we can't have an opinion on everything, we can on these certain things and take a position. If you're not at the table you are on the menu, as Andrew (Liveris) often says. You have to get involved in order to influence something. So, I feel so strongly, you just have to pick the things that align with your values.

In the vein of policy and politics, please elaborate a little on what IBM has done with Ivanka and the Pathways in Technology Early College High School (P-TECH) programs. – ***Andrew Liveris***

To give you a little background, you are all in a wonderful university. For whatever reason or whatever route, you are privileged to be in this program getting an education like this. P-TECH stems back to a belief we've had for a long time. Not through all of our history at IBM, but it really emerged as the digital era was growing. I felt you could see this big chasm happening between the haves and have nots, and it was happening in every country in the digital era. People were going to thrive in it, and then there were whole generations that were being left behind. A future no better than the past, even worse in some cases.

This was the background to P-TECH. And I want to make a really big point. If you're going to make technology, I think you have to bring it safely into the world. Safely means preparing society to use it. So whatever it is you are working on, it's the same. It does not just apply to tech companies, but to any company. So preparing society meant, okay, if artificial intelligence is going to impact every job, we better help people thrive and get good jobs, even if they don't have a college degree, and that's what got us down this path.

For all the focus on education, in the United States, 67% of people do not have a college degree or they're debt-laden with a college degree and don't have the necessary skills for a job. That's not a good position, and this is true in every country in the world. The percentages might be different, but this disparity is the same. At some point, you've got to do something that really matters. Work on something that matters – it is one of my life lessons about leadership. So this idea of preparing society, it became my passion. That we really could do something with our platform. So P-TECH started out with going to the most underserved communities, into high schools, community colleges or vocational schools.

The idea is, what if I went to a four-year high school or community college and I said, "Let me at least help you with curriculum. You'll be surprised. It's not hard skills, it's soft skills. And I'll give you IBMers as mentors; I will offer you a chance at an internship." We started this a decade ago, you got an associate degree and a high school degree at the same time, anywhere from zero to six years, as fast as you could move.

Today, we have 220 schools around the world, 150,000 kids coming through them. We're starting the program in Australia in about 10 schools as well. These were all first generation, the most underprivileged neighbourhoods, black communities and Hispanics mostly, or the poorest neighbourhoods in other countries. What did we find? Your socio-economic background does not determine your brains and so we found very able students who just needed help.

The second statistic to shock us was that 75% of these students go on to get four-year degrees. It's not what you expected. They have to work at the same time, so a little different situation because of their families, and then the next thing is they've grown like this. We ended up giving it a name, we called it 'new collar'. So, it wasn't blue collar, it wasn't white collar. We wanted to take away a stigma that if you didn't have a four-year degree to start, there was thought to be something wrong or bad about your skills.

Finally, the other side, and it's very much related to this moment, about growing inequality. The companies who hire had to change the most. We looked through every job record. In IBM they are all PhDs and four-year degrees, and we said is that true that every job really needs that to start? Because you're self-selecting out. You're not giving people a chance. And as we really pushed, we found 40% of our job requisitions could start without a four-year degree. You could be a cyber specialist, you could be a cloud engineer, and lots of other jobs.

Even more aggressively, it's taken me down this path. Because I believe to unite all of these communities, it is about giving people access to opportunity. Nobody wants a handout. This is about a chance to have a great job in this next era. I'm very passionate about this. This is squarely at the issue of giving people access to opportunity. I believe in it, so does Andrew (Liveris), and everybody agrees that this is the issue to address if you really want to make a systemic change.

I really admire what you just answered about giving everyone a shot, and I think it's led on from what we heard from Ajay Banga about decency quotient and giving everyone a level playing field. I am interested in your work in bringing the underserved and underprivileged into the workplace. What effect do you think that the Black Lives Matter movement, and also the rising unemployment rates in the United States, will have on hiring standards and diversity within the workplace? – *Scholar, Victoria Barnes*

Well, it's going to go one of two ways. It's either going to just be a passing moment that people go, well, and the next thing will come on, or we could really do something systemically to change. So, as an example, I'm part of a group that is going to try to build this coalition of companies. It's called OneTen, and it's a coalition to hire one million black employees into our companies over the next 10 years. Now, you may say one million is not a big enough number but, look, at least it is a start, and I am hopeful that what has happened will now create a permanent change.

I think IBM is a very inclusive company. In my surveys with my employees, 90% say it's inclusive. In 1899, IBM had its first Black employee. In 1940, a senior vice president was a woman. IBM had equality opportunities, 11 years before the civil rights movement ended. My first four managers were women, in the eighties. Thus, we think we're really progressive. However, during my tenure, societal issues started with diversity. We went on to inclusion and we were talking about equality, and now I'm talking about racial injustice. Something is wrong with this system! How did we go from that to this? That tells you something has been, at the core, wrong for a long time.

To address this, we started 'listening sessions'. We went out and talked to, up to maybe 3,000 or 4,000 of our Black employees. Every year we focus on a diversity group. This January we did the Black experience at IBM. Well, I thought, I think we need to do this, but I didn't know what I would hear. I'm going to marry this with what I then heard recently with the Black Lives Matter movement. So, our teammates stood up and bravely talked about their experience. These are very educated, very successful IBMers, and what they shared with the rest of the team was about what they felt their colleagues did not understand.

One, they feel the pressure to succeed is so high, that if they fail, they don't personally fail, they feel they ruin it for everyone around them and a generation to come. Or they ruin it for the country, for that matter. This is very interesting; I feel that somewhat for women, but I don't feel that for the whole of the universe. Then second, they said, "You don't realise the access most of you have." And they didn't mean access to a mentor, they just meant generally. The things that you're involved in, that they don't feel they get as much access to. So these two worlds.

Now, I'm going to fast forward to what happened after the killing of George Floyd in America. So we did these listening groups with all of our Black employees. We're talking thousands, highly educated, and I would say everyone can remember the day they were called a terrible name, and everyone can name multiple situations of being harassed, and harassed by the police. Everyone could talk to why they feel that they have to prove something more than others do. For instance, everyone has had to lecture their children about what to do if they are ever stopped by the police. That's heartbreaking to me.

I think when you see that so closely, I don't know how you can't permanently be changed. All the issues and solutions start at home. So, even in the company that I thought I was doing such a great job, I thought I can do a lot better. So we're going to do a lot better. Then, what you do focusses on a fair and equal opportunity, and you have got to help. As a result, this has become so vivid to me. The OneTen Coalition is a 10-year program. So this isn't something anyone fixes overnight, and therefore I'm so invested in these schools.

One of my greatest lessons of leadership for all of you is, one day, there will be a moment that you decide to work on something that matters. Now I encourage you to reflect, think about what will determine your future. It is schooling.

While a lot of us are lucky to get into a great school, that just isn't true for the majority.

> **Through your roles in IBM, you've been involved in partnering with some really big companies, and not just that IBM isn't big itself, but still these partnerships have grown IBM. What sort of leadership skills do you think are required so that you can get the most out of these partnerships and engage with other large companies? – *Scholar, Javan McGuckin***

Let me answer it two ways. One, I would say I have learnt from Andrew (Liveris), and that is, these have to be win/win partnerships. Any partnership that you just look out for, what is good for you but not the other party, doesn't work. Second, they have to be in service of the real client, otherwise there's no actual value. Third, partnerships are like relationships, it's what you do when no one is looking. Partnerships are what you really do and what it's based on.

So to recap, first and foremost, partnerships are around doing whatever you're in service of; if that's not clear, forget it. Then number two, it's got to be win/win, and number three, I never think a partnership is for show. They endure if both parties really put the effort into them, and it is what actually happens when no one is looking. For instance, you've experienced the results of Andrew's (Liveris) relationships this week. It's what Andrew does when no one is looking. It's his partnerships that are persistent.

Here's another great lesson. It isn't about looking at a partnership or a person as what they can do for you. If that's true, you'll get nowhere with a partnership or a relationship. So we started enterprise partnerships with Apple, as an example. That was one of the very big ones early on, and Apple was not very established in the enterprise, believe it or not, and they were really a consumer company. So, I believe we did our job. I mean, our value to them was to pull them into the enterprise, and with us they wrote a consumer gold standard. We were the enterprise gold standard; they were the consumer gold standard. So that was a win/win situation there. So, that's a bit of a trite statement, win/win, but I believe key partnerships to be enduring. If there's not value for both sides, it will not be good.

> **Can you please elaborate on another partnership, where sometimes out of a brave, courageous decision comes something successful? The one I'm referring to is to get out of semi-conductors and out of chip manufacturing that yielded an opportunity ultimately with Samsung. –** ***Andrew Liveris***

When you get to be my age and you get to reflect back, I always say all our revisions are history now, but there are lessons learnt. And one of them is don't protect your past, but know what must endure. Now, at this point in your career you're going to think that's such nonsense. Particularly if it's not a company you're creating, but it's a company that is going to change, and in this day and age they have to change so fast.

We really commercialised the semi-conductor industry. We owned it for 60 years. And to Andrew's (Liveris) point, we looked at it and said, "Okay, but now, in this world where semi-conductors go in everything – they're in your cell phones, they are the biggest import into China, 300 billion – and we're only making them for our high-end computers, that's it. We are a very tiny share of the market now." So, R&D is important, but not manufacturing, and we had to make a decision about these semi-conductors, but that was IBM's sacred cow for 60 years, and we were the originator of it. This has been true of many things.

So now we decided to say, look, it's got to go to the high-volume efficiency guys. We'll do the R&D part, and get a partner to do the development and manufacturing. But the big lesson to me was be willing to change everything but your soul, and to know what that is. I mean, I have found the days I got in trouble with IBM was because I got too far away from what really was our core business. Someone once said to me, be the best IBM, even in a change. Be your best IBM.

IBM is well known for R&D, so what makes IBM different, and what makes it more successful in this arena? – *Scholar, James Orman*

Well, first, most people have the D, they do not have the R, and be very careful to watch the difference between those two things: (a) they have two entirely different time horizons, they have very different investment mechanisms and (b) the biggest thing I would tell you that has made us different is an unwavering commitment to research that has never stopped. Through good, through bad, the worst of times, the best of times, we have hovered at about 6%. Six percent of our money has gone into R&D. It's never slashed. So, we're one of the few that's left with a really commercial research group.

The trick, as Andrew (Liveris) well knows, is how to commercialise research. There have been times we've gone, "Splitting a molecule, can I commercialise that?" Moving atoms to dance around and things like that. Okay, there's a certain point you say, I've got to at least take my research and be sure it can be applied. So that's always a spectrum you bounce back and forth in. But true research has a different horizon, and real breakthrough comes from it. So I am in favour of companies that maintain both those disciplines and do not integrate them into one thing, because I believe they are different.

When you asked what differentiates us, it's been an unwavering commitment to that. A belief that it is your down payment on the future. So it is quantum today. Quantum is a fairly popular topic in Australia if I remember from a recent visit. I believe we are the best quantum in the world in leading commercialisation, but that is on the shoulders of five decades of work. So, these time horizons will never line up here. So, I am a big proponent of them in being unwavering and committed to research for the long run.

You've got to have these verticals, deep verticals. There has to be a commitment to multiple-year spending that your shareholders will never reward you on, until they see the bottom line, especially these days. So the amplification of the R&D bet, like quantum, has to come with the commercial bet. Be willing to respect your past, but also to see the future and make the bet.

> **What do you see as being the next big breakthrough in artificial intelligence (AI), and also, what can we do as individuals to prepare ourselves for working in a world where AI plays such a big part? – *Scholar, Amber Spurway***

I believe the hope for AI is that it will help us solve lots of problems that we can't solve today. I'm positive about that. On the downside, I think it changes 100% of jobs, because I think it can do many things that we don't, and therefore the ethics around how it's used are really important. So let's just put this aside for a moment, this view that it needs to be ushered in safely, and AI needs to have ethics.

AI is a reflection of humanity. So it can be good, and it can be bad – you teach it. So, we won't go down that path again, but I'll just put that on the side. I am now seeing the things that it can do. For instance, when thinking of COVID-19 and our ability to understand medical conditions where several countries' call centres were overwhelmed. We did AI for 25 countries' call centres on medical questions over COVID-19. Therefore, it is really coming into its time.

At the moment, AI is used in only about 5% of processes. My view is because it's got to change the way we work. It is not like salt where you put it on something. It is not like a sprinkle of dust, and if you just try to dust it, put it on, you're never going to get your payback. You have to profoundly change how work is done, and that to me was the very biggest learning. The processes had to change, and if processes change, that means people have to change. Therein lies the problem of the speed at which AI will start to move.

I think a great example of this is what's just happened with education, and how long have we been talking distance learning? How long have we talked telemedicine? IBM made a huge bet on healthcare, and on paper, we could prove all the reasons and show the data why AI would be great, but you couldn't get people to change. Now, forced to in these last few months, boom, you see this explosion. So, it's got more to do about that, in my mind, and now I think we've broken through a few of those barriers because of the crisis, and those will now persist as we will go on, and I think you will increasingly start to see AI.

While you will all have to work with AI in your job, I have always believed it should augment you and make you better, not replace you. So if you go into it with the goal of I'm building this technology to replace people – not that you don't want efficiency – but AI, in my mind, is about making people better. This will allow AI to do the things you shouldn't be putting your brain power to and can complement you. There have been some outstanding AI examples because of COVID-19. People see this, and they're amazed. We had no choice with COVID-19. People had to go contact free, or they couldn't get as many people in the office. Suddenly, then, these things started getting adopted more. So, while I don't think this crisis may have necessarily created some new trends, it certainly accelerated ones that were there, and that's what you're seeing here.

You talk a lot about the two trillion dollar market for making better decisions, and I was curious where you see the technology for making better decisions being implemented in the future? – *Scholar, Megan Jones*

Our analysis shows that we're just 5% into the journey of really using things like AI and data to our benefit. Some reasons were technical, where things had to be made easier. In the beginning, it was just gruelling to do the teaching of these systems, but all that has become easier and easier. So, the technology had to be easier, the computer it ran had to be cheaper, and then you had to have us humans willing to change. There have been some things that pushed the latter one to happen now a bit more.

I think we are very early in chapter one for companies. With AI, most companies agree that they have random acts of digital and AI everywhere, which is very different to scaling a systemic change in your company. I can put up one little app and it does something, but I don't try to connect it to anything or make it do something bigger. That's where a lot of companies are right now, but they're stepping back. Like building a house, and they're saying, okay, no, no, no. Now, I see the promise so I've got to put the foundation in, and now I'm going to build on the foundation and put up a different kind of structure. So, that's where we are. That's why I say we're only really 5% into the journey of what AI can do for this world, and I think you will see it.

AI's got some natural places. For example, in customer care, it has got some processes that are natural in business that it can take care of, where you can adjudicate decisions. I think finally we may really breakthrough on healthcare. When you step back, a doctor is only correct about two-thirds of the time. Now, normally if I told you your AI was only right two-thirds of the time, you would say, "I am not putting that in. That's ridiculous." Your doctor is right two-thirds of the time, not the other third. So, these technologies could help that, right. For example, when reading mammograms, how many times do you think things are missed? These are the things that I think we're going to see a breakthrough on. I believe that AI with quantum computing could also be useful in relation to drug discoveries. My guess would have been about a decade ago, but soon we're going to see the bend of that curve.

> **You have bold leadership skills to do what is needed to be done for the IBM of this century, and you just talked about one or two of those. IBM is a company of around 350,000 people. It is not a start-up or a small company, so to make change you have to move this 'aircraft carrier' at the speed of light. As an example of such change, what was it like to do the 'gut check' on the decision to buy Red Hat and the pivot that was needed for a company of IBM's scale? – *Andrew Liveris***

Every company will have to reinvent themselves at some point, and we at IBM are 110 years old. The oldest of all the techs that are out there. So, everyone will come to terms with this. What people write about today is IBM's portfolio.

So today, 50% of the portfolio, which is $80 billion, is new in the last four to five years. So we've actually brought out new offerings. That's after divesting $10 billion of business. This represents things you have to part with, so you can make room to bring in the new, and we'd already done about 60 acquisitions before Red Hat.

Two parts of the story that don't get enough attention for any reinvention, has been more about how to change the way work is done, and then what new skills must people learn as the new currency. Regarding changing how work is done, this is very obvious to me. It is a world of consumerism and speed, and you have to build or put that in a large company, and you actually can engineer that. I always say to people, one of my biggest lessons learnt, I spent my first couple of years telling people, look you've got to go faster. This is obvious. The changes are obvious. Go faster, go faster. As I say, all I did was tire them out.

If you don't help 350,000 people do a job differently, they'll work very hard, but they'll end up with the same result. So, it led us down a journey of everything from agile workspaces; to co-location; to new tools; to Net Promoter Score; to all these kinds of things that you could build speed into something large. So, that is hard work to change the way people work and do their jobs.

The second part of that is their skills, like the ones you are getting in this Liveris program. I do really believe the future is about hiring people for their propensity to learn. The half-life of a skill in tech is three to five years. So if I hire you because you know one thing, and you've known it for a long time, the chances you want to learn a second one are not really high. So, if I want you, I'm going to hire you for curiosity. So, it's really related to that equal access and opportunity question. We have found all people test the same after a certain number of years. It didn't matter whether or not they had the four-year degree. If you really look at people's propensity to learn, it does not matter.

So, what led us to the largest acquisition in history of a software company? You get to a point, a tipping point, where it was very clear to me we were exiting chapter one of AI, and we were exiting chapter one of the cloud. What did they do in chapter one? They pretty much moved easy stuff, front ends. I could put a new little app on it. You could at least look at your airline reservation, maybe change a few things, maybe buy something. Don't get too far about rescheduling though. So, that's what all went on the cloud. Everything I call the experience side of life went on the cloud.

Chapter two though, Andrew (Liveris), why did IBM buy Red Hat? Chapter two was approaching to say, every company has got 80%. Any existing company who wants to reinvent themselves, this is hard work, and it's just like a home. You do not knock it down in one day. You don't get that pleasure. You've got to live in it while it's renovating, and so, this allowed people to look at what their house was and say, okay, leave the family room alone. We're going to rip out the kitchen, the bathroom is going to just get painted, and think about it with an application portfolio. I'm going to completely modernise these things, put it on this cloud. I'm going to leave this one just like it is, shrink wrap it, put a bow on it. That stays here. This one can go out on an

Amazon cloud. This has to be extremely secure, put it on the IBM cloud. That's a hybrid world, and that is a reality. That is about reinvention. That is the reality the world lives in right now when it comes to the cloud for business, and that is what Red Hat allowed us to do, and I think this is something you'll all easily understand. It gave the world a horizontal platform that if they wrote something once, they could run it anywhere they wanted.

Today, these are all islands. I build for Amazon, I can't move it anywhere. I build for Azure, it can't move anywhere. So, they actually became the IBM of the 1960s. A complete lock in, vertically, and that isn't innovation. The world wants open innovation. So the idea is, build once, run anywhere, take innovation from everywhere it comes. So that's why we were willing to spend on a $33 billion acquisition, because it's for chapter two of where this world goes with data, AI, and the cloud. The decision was educated. We nurtured, built, and developed the bridge to Red Hat and then I took it to the board so that we all understood, and we were holding hands together as we made that big bet. For any big bet you place, it's really about conviction.

From your experiences as a female CEO in a very male-dominated field, can you tell us a bit about your experiences, and if you have any tips for young women or men wanting to go into the entrepreneurial or business space? – *Scholar, Esandi Kalugalage*

Well, I'm going to quickly share a story, which is so illustrative of this point, Esandi. Probably 10 years into my career I was offered a job. A big promotion, and I told the person I wanted to go home and think about it, and I had to talk to my husband, who I am now married to for over 40 years. I remember going home and saying to my husband, I got offered this job, but I don't think I'm ready for it yet. I could do it better if I had about another year or so to get ready. Andrew (Liveris) knows Mark, my husband, and he sat there like he always does, listen, listen, listen, and he just said one sentence to me. Mark said, "Do you think a man would have answered it that way, told them he had to go home and think about it?" I said, "Probably not." And I went back in the next day, I took the job. My boss said to me, "Don't ever do that again." I said, "I understand what you are saying to me."

It was my most visceral understanding of something I've seen in my whole career, to this day: that growth and comfort will never co-exist. If you are going to learn and grow, you will take risks. I have found this to be most true for all my women colleagues. This inner doubt, which says if only I knew or if only I had just a little more, I could do this. Let me tell you the 10 reasons I can't do this, versus the 10 reasons I can. So my lesson from Mark was around growth and comfort. If you're going to grow, don't ever expect to be comfortable. So when I'm most agitated, I think this is good, I am really learning something, because that's what it means. If you can internalise that lesson, I honestly really believe that point of always putting yourself at some risk will mean that you will grow. Constantly look for opportunities that make you feel uncomfortable.

You've spoken about a few pieces of advice you were given throughout your career. What do you think was the most influential, which you'd give to others? – *Scholar, Simeon Gover*

There are two pieces of advice that are very relevant. Both have different time frames. One was from my mother. As Andrew (Liveris) knows, I was raised by a single mum. My dad left when I was 16. My brothers and sister were younger. He just left us, cold, no money, no home, food stamps, public welfare. My mother had never gone to college. Never had an associate degree. Hadn't actually worked a day in her life and had to find a way and she did. I would say I'm the underachiever of the family; my brothers and sister turned out fantastic.

Here's what my mum taught us, and it will apply to your whole life. It is that you should never let someone else define who you are. Only you define who you are. And it will be true for you as a person, and I think it will be true for the companies that you work for. I was reminded many times running IBM, if I didn't define what it was, somebody else would, and that's wrong. And it's true for yourself and it's true for your company. It's true at an individual level and many other levels. Only you define who you are, that would be one lesson.

The second one, I heard was a lesson from Napoleon that a colleague, Ken Chenault, said and it's a really great leadership lesson. He said the role of a great leader is to paint reality but give hope, and it is always this line you walk between those two. This idea has served me through the best of times and the worst of times. That you must be honest with people and paint the reality, but then your role is to give hope in that context.

So remember: only you define who you are and the leader paints reality and gives hope. Thanks to my husband, growth and comfort never co-exist, and the idea, that I hope you all do when you graduate – work on something that matters. It may not be immediate, but there will be a time your work will hit your heart, and it will become a passion for you. I hope you get to experience that feeling.

> **I recently read that IBM is stopping development of facial recognition technology. So I'm wondering, how does a big tech company like IBM create the balance between providing for its employees and shareholders and making ethical decisions, particularly in regard to privacy and surveillance? – Scholar, *James Orman***

To me, this is part of the definition of what it means to be good tech. There is a bifurcation in the world, and I hope we are a model for what good tech looks like. The reason we've endured over these number of years is because of trust. If you make decisions based on values, society, who gives you a licence to exist, in the end it is society that has allowed us to exist and that is because we've made value-based decisions, and that's a value-based decision that you decide on.

You won't do it in every single thing, right? You will pick your areas. But that is an area that we said, look, we're going to come down on the side of equality and justice, and this is an example that I can make. You can make your examples though your policy positions, through your product and in what you do with people.

In the end, it's about having enduring trust and that's why I said it's probably a fast one I can answer. To be trusted by society, trusted by your people, trusted by your clients. I am absolutely positive any company that has existed over 100 years, whether it is DOW, IBM, Johnson & Johnson, has done so because at some point, society decided, and continues to decide, to give us a licence to operate because of those kinds of decisions that we've made.

Scholar Reflection – Victoria Barnes

Ginni Rometty is the epitome of 'practice what you preach' and I was privileged to witness this firsthand from spending only one hour with Ginni. One topic that Ginni discussed frequently, and is very passionate about, is the idea that everyone deserves access to opportunity and to be able to show what they are made of. Since, as stated by Ginni, "your socio-economic background does not determine your brains". Ginni also emphasised that it is the responsibility of those who develop technology to bring it safely into the world by training society.

In fact, she has made this a reality for many underprivileged Americans with her initiative, P-TECH, which provides high school students with the opportunity to obtain a high school and associate degree at the same time. As I have been fortunate enough to have been given a philanthropic opportunity from the generous Andrew Liveris, I would love to follow Ginni's wisdom and be able pay it forward in the future, giving others the freedom to receive an education at a great university as well.

In the 21st century, technology is advancing at a rate never seen before. As such, some skills that were important 20 years ago might not necessarily be as relevant today. Ginni reiterated the importance of not hiring solely based on someone's degree, but rather their aptitude for hard work, creativity, soft skills and retrain-ability. I believe that changing the way we hire is an important lesson for leadership in the 21st century and directly links to giving everyone access to opportunity.

There were several lessons that I took away from listening to Ginni. However, my message to myself and other leaders would be these four key points. Firstly, you must operate like everyone is watching. Trust is a hard thing to earn but an easy thing to lose, and the decisions you make as a leader determines the level of trust that you have with society, your people and your clients. Secondly, regardless of who is in government at the time, "fight for what you believe in based on your values." Furthermore, "if you're going to grow, don't ever expect to be comfortable." Personally, I know that this statement is going to help me see differently the challenges I encounter, as well as helping me to pursue activities that will push me outside of my comfort zone. And finally, summarised perfectly by Ginni herself, "at some point, you've got to do something that really matters." So, I leave you with this question: what is the something you are going to do that really matters?

6

Human Rights Considerations and the Future of Work

Sharan Burrow

26th November 2020

To ensure human rights and climate action we must see reform of the business model. We have a group of people around the world who are indeed from different walks of life. From government, the United Nations (UN), civil society, and CEOs, including Andrew (Liveris) and myself, who have partnered in the B team (a global non-profit which advocates for business practices that are more centred on humanity and the climate) – to drive change. The world of work must shift, and these CEOs know that. They know that the norms of the economy must be in many ways re-written and yet it's very hard to actually change the dominant or orthodox patterns of people's lives. Insecurity is a deep fear for people.

In that context let me try to give you a sense of three

different but interrelated considerations. One is the state of the global labour market today. The second is the impact of COVID-19 on top of a pre-existing convergence of crises. And the third is some solutions; solutions that require dialogue to identify and implement.

The global labour market was indeed disintegrating before COVID-19. You all know about the massive inequality that we exist with today and that inequality has largely been generated by the nature of the business model that has been constructed. The nature of work, the nature of global trade, and of course the shareholder primacy as the foundation of the dominant quest for profit, influence the way corporations have been structured. This has been traditionally reinforced by a narrow definition of the legislation around fiduciary responsibility.

The construct of our supply chains is fundamentally dehumanising on several fronts. There is the search for production sites with cheap labour – exploitation with low wages and insecure, often unsafe work. Indeed 94% of the workers in supply chains are a hidden workforce to the CEOs of the major corporations that they make profits for as they are obscured behind multi-layered tiers of contracts. Then what many people don't realise is the fact that 60% of the world's labour force are actually working in informal work. This means no minimum wage, no rule of law, no social protection. And of course, not only is that affecting developing countries, but also migrants, and the unemployed who are desperate to survive through daily income.

It's also now characteristic of our new and emerging internet-mediated work arrangements. I know people call it 'the gig economy', though we prefer to use the term 'platform business'. The employment implications go way beyond the Ubers, and Deliveroos. It is actually about the breaking down of the traditional employment contract across many occupations.

And even then, for the 40% of workers in the formal economy who do have some form of employment contract, a third of those workers are in insecure or precarious work. You would have seen the campaigns, even in Australia, over the years against growing casualisation, the use of short-term contracts, and the insecurity of outsourcing.

Governments have failed in their responsibility for regulating labour markets, often influenced by the lobby of big business. This means a lot of people feel very insecure about work even before we get to the enormous questions of 'just transition' for climate and technology change affecting the future of work.

As an example, while you may have direct employment in a German company with best practice in terms of responsible industrial relations; an employer and employee works council so there's constant consultation; co-management through corporate advisory boards with trade union representation; collective bargaining which sets decent wages and conditions by agreement – the reality is this is limited to the domestic workforce with some spillover throughout Europe where the law requires. There is no equivalent responsibility for each tier of contracting whether from companies from Germany, Belgium, the Netherlands, Australia, the United States or wherever the companies are headquartered. The absence of responsibility for workers in supply chains means we are very far from realising Goal 8 of the United Nations Sustainable Development Goals on decent work and full employment.

As already cited, 94% of the Asia-Pacific supply chains are a hidden workforce for which there is deficit in decent work, and it varies by only a percent or two in other regions. That's a pretty devastating indictment of corporate management. In large part it is why the social contact has been broken. This is at odds with the intent of the origins of the global rule of law defining the social contract. Following the First World War, the conflict was so socially devastating that government leaders with workers and their unions joined forces and also invited the business community to establish the International Labour Organisation (ILO) which to this day establishes, through tri-partite negotiations, the global standards for the world of work. There are many standards, but the Fundamental Principles and Rights at Work include freedom of association or the right to join a union, the right to collective bargaining, to be free from discrimination and the elimination of child and forced labour. Now with the exposure through the pandemic of the importance of workplace safety, the addition of established occupational safety and health standards to the list of these fundamental rights and standards is being considered.

In addition to the ILO Constitution, if you want to read one document that depicts the origins of the commitment to a rights-based social contract, then read the Declaration of Philadelphia, from 1944. It's a very brief document, but it covers the fundamentals of decent work. The document discusses minimum living wages, the rule of law, social protection, and social justice. Indeed, after two world wars and the Great Depression this was the foundation of the social contract which underpinned recovery and subsequent development for industrialised nations.

Then the 1980s saw the beginning of hyper-globalisation and the explosion of massive global supply chains underpinning the global economy. If you consider labour income share from this period until today it's a relatively constant downward spiral – like a roller coaster. It continues to go down despite the world being some four times richer in gross domestic product (GDP) terms than it was in the 1980s.

That's the situation that already existed when COVID-19 hit. Along with this massive inequality we also had the crisis of climate and the loss of lives and livelihoods through climate emergencies.

Australia knows firsthand the devastation of bushfires, floods, cyclones and tsunamis, with the increasing frequency of these extreme weather events driven by climate change. Tragically we have not seen either crisis addressed effectively in Australian public policy to date. However, this was the social and environmental backdrop which the impact of COVID-19 has exposed and deepened.

In 2020, 250 million jobs were lost and at least a further 130 million are at risk in 2021. Additionally, the global health crisis has shone a spotlight on the frontline workers, mainly women, who we depend on yet who are amongst the lowest paid. Equally the underfunding of both health and other sectors of the care economy have been exposed and must be addressed. Consequently, both national and global challenges for recovery and resilience are serious and require reforms in many areas of both public policy and business practice.

This must also be the backdrop for when people talk about the future of work. Inclusive growth requires integrated solutions. There is a lot of focus on the innovative end of the curve. How is technology changing the work? How are we working digitally? What does that mean for the future? We can explore these and other questions, but in order to address these it's critical to look at the whole picture.

Governments have failed to regulate the market in almost all countries. It's been an ongoing contest between the rule of law with the rights of people and security versus the corporate model that has dominated public policy and regulation. This has largely been the American corporate model because it is very anti-union, anti-environmental standards and very committed to profit at any cost. It is at odds in many ways with the European social model. In fact, Europe right now is repairing its social model. They're going through huge debates about a social pillar of rights to repair and build for the future on the foundations of previous social foundations.

So, what are the solutions? In 2019, even before the pandemic, the ILO with business, employers and worker representatives, negotiated the Centenary Declaration on the Future of Work which outlines the solutions for human-centred recovery. For workers, the agreement to a labour protection floor for all workers would help repair the labour market, with fundamental rights, occupational health and safety, an adequate or evidence based minimum wage and maximum hours of work.

These elements of the social contract must be married with universal social protection, a transformative agenda for the inclusion of women and 'just transitions'. Progress for women has stalled on every indicator, and participation of women in the workforce is going backwards with the majority of the 80 million workers who dropped out of the labour market last year being women. 'Just transitions' is a commitment now written into the Paris Agreement and accepted more and more globally. It's not about whether we deal with climate action because there must be transition in every economic sector when the very existence of human lives are at stake. But 'just transitions' for climate and for technology are important to ensure the security of jobs and decent work and thus build the trust of working families to support these vital changes. We cannot have stranded assets but equally we cannot have stranded people or stranded communities.

At the same time, technology change is driving change faster than at any time in our history. The unions have never been opposed to technology. In fact, while technology can cause displacement, just as transition for climate is causing displacement for some sectors and must be mitigated for those workers, technology in many circumstances can also secure a better future. It all depends on the way it's adopted and that can't be governed by technological determinism. Australian unions have traditionally used technology to upskill workers and to increase skilled wages. Unfortunately, that element of collaboration has broken down in too many areas. So, when new technologies threaten jobs through automation or digitalisation we need to look at what constitutes a 'just transition' for the workforce, just as we need to do with climate.

And there are new and emerging laws already. Legislation has been passed in both Spain and Argentina as a floor of what remote working through telework should be based on. There is the hope of the United Nations Guiding Principles on Business and Human Rights (UNGPs) with 'due diligence'. This is risk analysis of human and labour rights violations and must be accompanied by grievance procedures at all levels to effectively remedy. When accompanied by continuous monitoring of supply chains, due diligence can help clean up our supply chains.

Ten years in maturity, those UNGPs are widely accepted but there is still no broad-based implementation. There are however positive legislative developments. There's a United Nations treaty being negotiated, and we've got the mandated 'due diligence' laws in France and Germany. Five other European countries were considering legislation but now the European Union (EU) has said it will mandate 'due diligence' right across the board. That will change the base of the trade landscape because you won't be able to trade in and out of Europe if you don't comply and therefore this will affect corporate global supply chains. It will also add to that floor a guarantee for rights and environmental standards through mandated corporate responsibility.

In the absence of legislative action by government, corporations themselves can take the initiative to act. I won't talk about how to implement 'due diligence' because there's a range of models, including union partnerships through direct employment and supply chains. There is also terrible practice with outsourcing auditing. But the world of work is shifting slowly but surely to implementation of some positive measures for people and the planet.

We cannot build an inclusive future with shared prosperity without a fair competition floor that ensures respect for human rights, labour rights and environmental protection.

Could you expand on what opportunity you see emerging as a result of both COVID-19, but also the current political situation globally, and what can we do to ensure we make the most of these? – ***Scholar, Amber Spurway***

So, it depends where you're looking for opportunities, Amber. For me, I'm looking at opportunities to actually put a floor of rights and security under workers, which is emerging largely in Europe. That's where the debate's going on. From the breadth of the debate to say how do we go beyond GDP to measure wealth, through to the questions of, as I said, 'due diligence' of skills training of the sort of income guarantees that people need and redeployment support if their jobs are displaced, or indeed they need to upskill workers.

So if I took a company like Danone, for example, who have shifted from that dominant shareholder model to a model of 'Entreprise à Mission', which is a public benefit company that actually looks at the interests of all of its stakeholders. Then they say that in this difficult time, anywhere in the world, they won't lay off workers who earn under about €35,000; they will re-skill them and look for other areas. So there are opportunities to rebuild a sense of responsibility for the workforce. But there are also opportunities around building the rule of law.

In terms of the way people work, then there are opportunities in this virtual world, there's no question about that. The reach is broader, you can work globally from Australia, and even in an environment where you may never get to travel for the next couple of years. Although I think we have got some solutions now for the world of travel, I don't think anyone will go back to actually saying that the constraints in some jobs, in professional jobs, are limited by geography. Although you may be required for face-to-face meetings from time to time.

Of course, working from home gives you more flexibility about where and who you work for. However, I can also say that the downside of working from home is indeed extraordinary, the levels of mental health problems are going through the roof. There's no way – you know I manage 150 staff – and there is no simple way to make sure your staff aren't isolated, that their productivity isn't diminished. For some it goes up, for others it goes down because they don't cope well. Indeed, working from home seems like a dream for a working mother, but try juggling children and work. And of course, domestic violence when both partners have been locked down has gone through the roof because as people lose their jobs the tension is extraordinary, or just incredible tension of having two working adults, children, lack of money, whatever it is in the house – unacceptable. But in human terms, you can look to the causes without too much difficulty. So yes, there are definitely opportunities.

Companies are restructuring and they're looking, the ones that I think are going to be ahead of the pack, are looking much more at a local environment and how they manufacture or respond to the domestic market, rather than simply looking from countries like Australia, or in Europe or wherever, to the developing world as one-way traffic. Where we produce in low-cost countries, low-wage countries, and we transport to the world.

There's a tremendous shift going on, but also where we invest in jobs. Because that's an enormous opportunity. Of course we need infrastructure, we need to reinvest in industry policy for smart manufacturing. We need to look to our agricultural security. There are jobs in all of these areas as we start to rebuild the economy. But if you look at the facts, we've underfunded 'care' – health, education, childcare, aged care. There are really good jobs in care, but for women there's also the capacity then to have that burden of care lifted with those supports and take part in the broader labour market. So yes, if we get the floor right, there are huge opportunities.

Regarding a global labour protection floor that you're proposing, with disparities in culture and lifestyle and our modern reliance on quick, cheap labour outsourced through supply chains through periphery countries or underdeveloped countries. How is it actually possible to establish a unified global protection floor and actually see the implementation of that? – *Scholar, Lilly Van Gilst*

Well, I'm not going to pretend it's easy work. I'll give you two examples. When I took over this job 10 years ago – my God, do I feel ancient these days, and that 10 years has seen incredible eruptions in the world – I did what we would describe as due diligence. I wanted to understand, because I came from a small country like Australia, I had worked in international roles but in a voluntary sense, but I still didn't really have a grasp of the world of work in every country.

So, we did our due diligence, and to my horror I found that in the Gulf states (i.e., Middle East), some of the richest countries in the world, they were basing their development model on cheap labour, mostly from Asia, but are into Africa now, and it was basically modern slavery. You were owned effectively by one other person. You paid to get a job. Sometimes your employer would pay for the flights, but poor workers went into incredible debt, arrived in places like Qatar to actually find that their contract was false, it would be torn up. They'd be paid half the wages. They depended on accommodation, on the very legal assistance to be there, and then of course they couldn't even leave the country without permission of the employer.

So, it took us five or six years of an incredibly difficult campaign, but then the government decided they would negotiate, and we used everything. I walked those labour camps, documented the squalor and the deprivation of workers, and ultimately, we also used the leverage of the World Cup being there in 2022, the Football World Cup. Then there was a complaint at the ILO and we negotiated with government, and now just this year we've seen all the laws in place.

All that floor I talked to you about is in place. There's social protection, there are minimum wages, there's now a rule of law, and there are labour courts. We built labour courts with the help of some of my Australian Fair Work Commission contacts and others around the world and that's now. There's a couple of other things still being rolled out, but the rules are there. There is in fact an advisory structure, there are selected committees in every country.

I'll tell you about another country, which is Bangladesh, where it's not a system of slavery, but it is a system of exploitation. The textile sector is enormous in Bangladesh and it's been absolutely decimated by the lockdown and the shutdown of enterprises because of COVID-19. So the employers and ourselves and everybody has been working to see what we can do in Bangladesh. But even as we're trying to rebuild those jobs, we are also looking at how to clean up their labour laws. Because there's been a long period of exploitation and the government wanted to attract all that fast fashion investment. So, of course, it wasn't regulating in the interests of its people.

However, just last week, after a union campaign, we're about to start negotiations on a roadmap with Bangladesh. The roadmap is to uncover how they get their labour laws to exactly the point that you ask. So, I'm not going to pretend it's easy, because Indonesia is going the other way because they're so worried about the current environment and the impact of COVID-19. They've shifted some of those basic securities for their workers out of the legislative world, and they say openly to attract foreign direct investment. That again will become a tremendous struggle in Indonesia, but that is the way of the world.

That's why if we get that mandated due diligence, if we get a UN treaty, then that will shift some of the issues with local worker protections. Because all foreign direct investment, if it wants to trade in and out of places like Europe, or if there's a UN treaty much more globally, countries will have to actually follow a different rule of law. So, it's possible. That's why unions exist, because if you can't build on the collective power of unions to oppose exploitation or modern slavery or other areas of oppression, then you can't change the face of the world.

This is like young people and the climate debate. The mobilisations of young people for climate has been extraordinary and it has really given a shift for those of us who've been campaigning for climate change. Because we don't have a choice for a 'just' transition. So, I hope you'll join the ranks of young people mobilising for a better future because you can shape the world at work, no question. It's about staying the distance, working out what you think is just, and maintaining the momentum.

I would just say one other thing in terms of your question, that the supply chains are changing. If you look at just one technology, digitalisation, really that's one tiny kind of sliver off the top of the economy if you like. Forty percent of the world's people still aren't connected to the internet, and of course those supply chains are still in existence whatever the dominant demand – for fast fashion, fast food, or just-in-time manufacturing. But if you actually look at 3D printing, that is already shifting at least some of the high-end of manufacturing back onshore in major countries. So again, the only model that would be a successful model to balance that is development in terms of multi-national companies seeing themselves as producers for the domestic market and formalising jobs. So, there's a lot of work to do.

What are the roles of governments, companies and individuals in ensuring a 'just transition' to a low carbon future? – *Scholar, Flynn Pearman*

It's a great question. It takes up a lot of my working life, because clearly we've had many transitions. You've heard us talking about some of the worst of them this morning. But if you look, even in Australia, and look to the demise of the car industry, for example, or other transitions, then not all of them have been done well. So when we were trying to turn around the consciousness of people, you have to go back almost 15 years when the debate was on in the international world of labour, workers and the unions, around why we needed to change.

I actually read my first Intergovernmental Panel on Climate Change (IPCC) report in 2000. I'd just taken over as the president of the Australian Council of Trade Unions (ACTU), and it was like reading a horror story and I've read them every year since. They haven't gotten any better, but by 2002 in Australia, we were talking about how this would be the biggest systemic shift in the world of work and that we had to be out in front of the curve.

Now, have we got there? Not particularly, Australia has had terrible contentious debates across all sectors of the community and into government about this. But in other countries we have got there, and so we coined the campaign, 'just transition'. We got it in, we missed out of course, because of the collapse of the Copenhagen Agreement. Lost a number of years. Got it into the Paris Agreement in 2015, and now we've campaigned and continue to campaign everywhere to get it in governments' Nationally Determined Contributions (NDCs) – what commitment they're going to make as a country.

We campaign everywhere to get environmental standards, and due diligence aligned. What it requires is 'just transition' measures. Now, 'just transition' measures are very simple if you really break it down. They're about making sure older workers are protected should their jobs be displaced or changed. That older workers who are probably going to be the most affected actually have secure pensions. Sometimes there's three, five, seven years to the pension, and workers may choose to retire. So, you need bridges to pensions. Then you need, for younger workers, you actually need to make sure that the income support, the skills development support, or the re-skilling, and redeployment support is there in a package that gives people security and hope.

There are countries like Denmark and Sweden that have done this very well. No one would be out of a job in Denmark or in Sweden for over seven or eight months, and in that period they would in fact be being supported to re-skill, and they'd be having redeployment support. But most nations don't do this well at all.

Then it's about the renewal of community, because we've seen many transitions devastate communities. And that's the fear that you see around the coal debate in Queensland

and other parts of the world. If you talk to coal miners, and I've walked the coal fields of countries around the world and it's painful. It's really painful. I mean, these are great communities, built off this industry. They're strong. They commit to the economy, and they're good secure union jobs, but people recognise that the future will be different. It's just that the insecurity is holding back that trajectory. So unless you have a dialogue with employers and dialogue with governments to make it possible to make that shift, then it is going to be contested. It will be bloody, in the truer sense of the word, as you've seen in political contests and community contests in Australia.

Globalisation has increasingly been found to be linked to inequality in work, both within and between countries. So, do you think that inequality can ever be really reduced without cutting down on globalisation? – ***Scholar, Esandi Kalugalage***

Well, that's a good question. Inequality can be reduced, no doubt, but it has to change the model of globalisation. And the changing globalisation is going to be more dramatic because of climate and the need to reduce emissions, and where we produce goods, and whether we eat food that's from thousands and thousands of kilometres away, or whether we look to our hundred mile, thousand kilometre, whatever it is, radius of production as a dominant supply. A whole range of things are changing with people's choice.

But can we reduce inequality? Absolutely! Look at that distribution curve of income, and you put a minimum income, a minimum evidence-based basic income. And by the way, in those dehumanising supply chains, our work shows that it would take less than $50 USD a month extra to actually bring those workers in the poorest of Asian countries up to a minimum living wage, to very basic wages. But that would give people the hope of survival. And when you look at the profits of companies, then I can tell you that is absolutely affordable. So, we can do something about inequality.

We can look at the social protection base of people who fall out of work, don't have enough work, and make sure everybody has a basic income if they do not have work. That actually gives them that sort of security of survival. But in terms of what you said about whether it would decrease globalisation or increase it, you know, I don't think fixing inequality would decrease globalisation. In fact, if we change the development model, which has really kept the developing countries poor, and shared trade and global prosperity more, we would probably see quite a massive increase. Not necessarily good for the planet, although if we get the circular economy right we can manage that as well, but developing countries will see a lot more optimism for their own future and that of their children.

If we actually look at the slump of global demand now, it has nothing to do with profits. If you look at the big tech companies, then they've increased their profits by 41% just to June this year through the pandemic. Probably double that by the end of this year. Sadly, they're not paying fair tax, they're treating their workers very badly and the global monopoly is not good for fair competition for the rest of the community, the rest of the real economy. So, we're also looking at all those laws. How you break them up, what are the new taxes, like a digital tax, and so on.

So, will globalisation be reduced if you do something about inequality? To give you a sense of what it would mean in fast fashion to pay that extra $50 or even $100 a month. You know, for a T-shirt it might be between $1 and $3. So, I don't think it's going to affect demand because of price. I think the demand in the world will be affected by a whole range of other factors. To be honest, doing something about inequality is just a matter of political will.

Are you able to elaborate on how countries can reform their social contract to allow for a more inclusive growth without causing a huge upheaval in the way things currently stand? – *Scholar, Simeon Gover*

So, for the International Trade Union Confederation (ITUC), the global union movement, we have several pillars. In fact, I just held our General Counsel virtually with people from all around the world for the last two days and we reinforced there are four pillars which form the foundation of our work. One is peace, democracy and rights. The other is regulating economic power. The third is global shifts and 'just transition'. So again, climate and technology in the main. The fourth is equality and inclusion.

From these pillars, we draw three frontline public campaigns where we take the critical areas from each of those pillars and construct frontline campaigns. So, one is the new social contract. The second one is climate and climate-proofing our workplaces and our future. So how do you drive employment but manage the climate challenge as well? Then, there's a 'just transition' factor that underpins all that and the third is actually rebuilding trust in democracy.

I don't know if you'd be surprised at this or not, but less than 50% of people live in democracies today. And in our world, you can't achieve either of those two frontline ambitions if you don't have democratic countries where people can actually have a say about the priorities. The really tragic figure is that less than 45% of young people actually believe in democracies. Whereas in the 1970s and 80s it was double that. So, we've got to rebuild democracy but on a very different scale.

When you look to New Zealand, for example, they have actually already gone beyond GDP. They have government transparency and accountability across a range of areas. That goes to jobs, livelihoods, people's rights, the environment and so on. So that's our third area, rebuilding trust in democracy. Because if you don't have that, it's very hard to affect the other two.

Just to give you a sense of how unions play out in that, take the United States' unions who campaigned right around the country to affect the election outcome in the United States. In a very poor country, Somalia, which hasn't seen universal franchise or voting for around 50 years, they have a campaign about Somalia, to encourage voting – *Let's Talk Elections.* But even in the current context, they've achieved the first step which is to expand the voting college. Now they are campaigning to build a manifesto from the ground up with their members through technology. It's amazing in

Somalia, which is a war-torn country, as you know. Very courageous trade unions we have there.

If you look at your question about reforming the social contract – for instance, in Australia you have the elements in place. Whether they are adequate or not, is really the contestation, but in Australia you do have a minimum wage, you do have collective bargaining rights. They have been stripped back so that they are not as effective as the standard would allow, but you do have collective bargaining rights. You have maximum hours of work, although they're breaking down, as you know, and you have occupational health and safety laws. So that floor exists in Australia. Has it been weakened by constant attacks from government?

At the same time, you are way too young to remember, but we fought a massive campaign, you know, how many years ago? We campaigned from 2005 to 2007 to defeat the worst of those laws which would have broken down that social contract totally. Still contestable, but it's there. For women, a lot more work is necessary, the inclusion of women. Australia has done some great work around equal pay, particularly in the community sector, but you can still see the difference.

Now for climate and technology, you know, there are people campaigning for a 'just transition' authority. It's absolutely vital, but if you put that in place, and if you make sure our tax base is recovered, then we look at the new taxes Europe is looking at, digital tax, a wealth tax or a billionaire's tax. There are more billionaires in the world now. Jeff Bezos is the richest man in the world, and he earned an additional $70 billion through the pandemic; he's now worth about

$180 billion or something. Now you can't spend that money in a lifetime. So even if you had what we call a billionaire's tax, you give some back to the community to pay for that health, climate transition, care and education, the deficits and so on. So is the basis of Australia's social contract intact? Yes, but does it have to be repaired? Absolutely!

> **There seem to be major benefits in implementing sustainable technology, both scientific and with jobs. So, I'm curious as to why you think we're not seeing a faster and greater shift to this new state? Also, what are the major challenges that you have personally experienced in trying to convince people for this 'just transition'? – *Scholar, Victoria Barnes***

It has been one of the most difficult campaigns I've taken on in my lifetime. But you know, you start from an excellent base. Let me give you the positive story first. Overwhelmingly, our global polling shows people know that it's necessary and want urgent climate action – we're talking 79% of people. It's not like people don't accept the science, but if you think about the dominant power of wealth, and the foundations of all of our industrial base, which has been the backbone of economies, then the fossil fuels industries have driven those.

So, who are the biggest opponents? The fossil fuel companies. Now, they also create fear for workers because they don't want to transition. Coal's in a different space. There's nothing you can actually do with coal. It's a little bit like saying we want to save your telephone exchanges – your grandparents would remember. When I grew up in a small rural town in New South Wales, going to work on the telephone exchange, where when somebody called in on one line, you take the plug and put it in another one – you've probably seen it in the movies. That was a good job for a young woman, leaving school in those days. It was a good, secure, unionised job that doesn't exist anymore.

You have the amazing technologies that we have today. So, transitions have happened everywhere in our lifetime, and coal's is painful. So yes, if I walk the coal fields with these coal mining unions, it will break your heart because of the solidarity and the generosity of coal mining unions and the workers. They have built communities right throughout Queensland, throughout New South Wales, throughout Western Australia and other places. They were absolutely the backbone of rural communities, and the backbone of an industry. Very painful but there will still be energy workers.

The question is, what kind of energy will they work in? For example, if you look at Denmark, it's built a wind industry that it now exports, and all those jobs are unionised. They're good jobs. But at the moment, around the world, when people look at moving from fossil fuel jobs to energy jobs that are in renewables, then the wages and conditions are very different. So, it's our job, and frankly the responsibility of government and employers, to see that we can make that transition.

As much as transitioning from coal is painful, there are communities in Australia that have taken that on like Port Augusta in South Australia where they built the closest thing to coal fired power stations, which are solar thermal power plants to transition workers. Now the timing was wrong, but there are ways of transitioning energy workers that make it possible for good jobs in energy. My total frustration with the fossil fuel companies is on two fronts. One is that they have the power and the platforms and the technologies to transition, but they are doing it so slowly. Such a small amount of capital expenditure into renewables compared to fossil fuels and now of course they are trying to hang on with expanded gas. Gas was always going to be a transition technology, but not new gas. So those debates are everywhere now, and of course whether it's clean or dirty hydrogen.

The energy transition is possible. It's just whether we're going to see the dominant voice of companies dictate government policy and frustrate the transition or accelerate it. I'm an optimist by nature, and even though that's a really tough battle, I think we will get there, particularly with many of the European fossil fuel companies. The other beef we have with them is that it's possible for them to change the aviation fuel mix, but these fossil fuel companies won't change because it is the dominant profit stream for them. Now, ultimately, they will because regulation will change. But it could be much faster without the opposing voice of big capital. It's that simple.

I read an article quoting some ITUC 2017 figures that said that 85% of the world's population wants the rules of the global economy to be rewritten. So, how can we take people who just want this and turn them into people who actively work towards it? – *Scholar, James Orman*

That's a good question. Well, you know I'm going to throw it back to you because we know that convergence of the four crises I talked about right now: (1) inequality, (2) exclusion of women but also race, treatment of migrant workers, etcetera, (3) the questions of climate, and now (4) the health crisis. When you look at all of those, we may have a framework for solutions, but it's going to be a struggle of the generations.

So, we initiated intergenerational dialogues within the union movement. I'm going to hold the first intergenerational debate between a union leader and Fridays for Future student activists in several countries around 'just transition' and climate very soon. I'm really looking forward to that, and there will be an Australian student and a labour leader who will be part of that conversation with me. So, I think it's really about the dialogue, people must talk about these things together across the field. I'm totally committed to engagement with people of all ages, but in all parts of our society as well.

Unless people feel secure, feel like they've got a voice, feel like they're part of a dialogue, then of course you will not affect that change. But you're right about one thing, it takes activism, because going back to the power of democracy, if you want to change something, the most powerful element for change is still the power of people at the ballot box. And then of course there is political engagement through activism and through dialogue. All sorts of structures, and many countries are now playing with different kinds of democratic engagement, beyond the ballot box. So, you are seeing citizen juries or citizen discussion groups often sponsored by government.

Looking at what are the solutions to intractable problems, we're going to need a lot more of that because people have the answers. It's not like we're not smart. I mean, we're more educated than we've ever been in our lifetime. It's just that people don't actually talk about it. So, some things you'll be engaged in, in that activist sense, is what do you do about surveillance? What do you do about privacy? How do you protect your privacy online when you're actually an internet generation?

People often say, well, you know, there's nothing we can do about that. Well, there's actually a lot you can do. I sit on the supervisory body of the Centre for the Fourth Industrial Revolution, where you get all the technology CEOs. All the people, whether it's in the United States from Silicon Valley, or whether it's in India, or whether it's in China. And these are the things they talk about more than the actual technology, because they know that's the risk of our future, a cyber future versus the technology itself.

We need young people as activists pushing people in jobs. But I always have one piece of advice for anyone who wants to take on a cause. Just do it. Don't assume you need a position, because power is not constructed by labels alone. If you build a group of voices and use the collective power of a voice around a local or a national issue, then you will have an influence. And again, I come back to the Fridays for Future contingent, when the students decided they were going to mobilise. It's been a joy to be honest, but it's been a game changer for people who have been trying to point out – from the scientists through to environmental organisations, to unions – that we needed action on climate.

So good luck, I hope to see you somewhere in the future where I'm cheering you on as a young activist.

> **I recall you talking about a UN treaty, so I was wondering how you think we can make sure that that is stuck to or comes to fruition? Because it's a human right to seek asylum by the UN, but that doesn't stop human right abuses. – *Scholar, Megan Jones***

That is a very good question. But if you didn't have the UN Declaration of Human Rights, if you didn't have the ILO standards, then we would have no basis for the rule of law, and you would be back to an incredibly lawless set of society. So yes, if you go back to that democracy figure, where you've got less than 50% of people living in democracies, then we have some real challenges. But even in those democracies, you're absolutely right; the asylum, the refugee debate is one that still breaks my heart. It's front and centre for me personally but also in my role in Australia, and when I go to refugee camps or walk amongst migrant communities seeking asylum or seeking work and residency in other countries, it's really heartbreaking. It's extremely heartbreaking and it is absolutely against the rule of law. However, that's why that activism and vigilance of a democratic society is essential for us to change the rules and then to maintain them.

So if we get a UN treaty, which I'm optimistic we will, it's really interesting about how people who ignored this are now having arguments with me about, "Well, did you see which governments initiated them?" I'm saying, "What does it matter? Like, what does it matter which governments initiated it? Get in there and help us negotiate for a rule of law that will be fair competition for business. So, they can win while guaranteeing due diligence and rights for working people and, in a broader human rights context, for people in the community."

So, the EU coming on board is going to help enormously. They weren't negotiating at all. Now the EU is in the negotiations, and now with their commitment to due diligence, I'll have a negotiating mandate. We think it will take the next couple of years on the treaty negotiation. Unlike the ILO, the UN treaty, if it takes a decade, that's a short time to negotiate a UN treaty. Whereas in the ILO we can negotiate new standards of law in two years, and over two sessions in two years. So it takes effectively six weeks over two years with a lot of work behind the scenes.

Sometimes it takes 10 years to build a campaign. So, when we got a convention for domestic workers, it took 10 years in campaigning, two years to affect it. Same thing for the other convention we won last year, which is elimination of violence. It started off as violence against women, but in the end it became even more inclusive and we were campaigning for the elimination of violence in the workplace. Of course, that's very pointed now with the increase in domestic violence and so on at home, which is your workplace during COVID-19.

So first, get a rule of law, and then you have to be vigilant. I've been known to say 'it's about rules and fear' – or 'vigilance' is a nicer word – but it is. You know, rule of law is only as strong as the people who are committed to it and committed to seeing justice prevail. So, it's like the last discussion, you cannot get away from the fact that building a just future will take both. You need activism with vigilance and you need the rule of law; and of course you need some good luck!

Over the course of your career, how has your perspective changed on what leadership is and what makes an effective leader? – *Scholar, Javan McGuckin*

I'm really bad on the leadership questions because I'm an accidental leader. I was a teacher, and that was the beginning of my professional working life. I loved being a teacher, never expected not to be a teacher, but I was also very committed to my trade union because, you know, for the Teachers' Unions it was both sides of my heart. One side was quality of teaching for students, and the other side was decent work for the teachers themselves. So, when my union asked me to step out and do a job for a few months at one point in my teaching career, I did. After a bit of to-ing and fro-ing, the rest is history.

I just happened to be in the right place at the wrong time or something. And of course, if you're open to opportunities, then those opportunities can come along. But I have a firm belief that leadership is not about title. If you look at some of the incredible leaders in our world, it's people who've taken on matters of injustice or areas of the rule of law or whatever it is with no title, but with a commitment, and they have built a community of activism and demand from that. And then of course it's shaped by leaders in the law, in parliaments, in unions, whatever the range of institutions are.

I think leadership is about understanding the world you're working in. Feeling very strongly about something and deciding you're going to stand up and then looking at who else will stand up with you. Then you need to define what the skills and strategies are that you need to campaign for change. So, I always tell women that as much as we run leadership courses, don't wait for the title. Whatever you're passionate about now, take it on, and actually make yourself the voice of reason around change and people will gather behind you, or with you.

I have the most privileged job in the world, you realise. Again, quite by accident. But I can go into any country, walk through any workplaces, call up any employer where I see an injustice, and decide that something's so bad that I'm going to make trouble – anywhere in the world. But then I also have a responsibility to settle that dispute and to make sure that we leave the foundations of justice, whatever they might be, in place for the people who were in fact the victims of oppression. So, that's a pretty incredible thing and they pay me to do it and that will be something that I will treasure for a lifetime. So just put yourself out there, think about opportunities, and take them up when they come if they suit what you want to do.

Scholar Reflection – Esandi Kalugalage

I had been very excited to hear Sharan Burrow speak to us ever since learning about her passion and drive to ensure women around the world overcome barriers within their communities for independence and in the workplace for rights and equal opportunity. Not only is this topic close to my heart, I was eager to hear her opinions on climate change, the world's labour market and globalisation, as someone with decades of experience in an international people-based leadership role.

Sharan spoke about the necessity to stabilise the world's labour market – particularly given the impacts on developing countries and the revealing correlation between income inequality and globalisation. I enjoyed her point about the much-needed reformation of the social contract both on a national and global level.

Perhaps the idea that resonated most with me during Sharan's talk was her passionate view that it is up to young people to mobilise together, when concerned about the state of the world and seek to make a visible difference. She offered a piece of useful advice: "If you want to take on a cause just do it, don't assume you need a position, because power is not constructed by labels alone." Personally, it was empowering to hear someone in Sharan's high leadership level say this to us.

Hearing Sharan speak about the importance of every person in mobilising to create change reminded me about the core aspect of leadership: leading yourself and others to make a part of the world a better place. Often, I find myself getting lost in the specifics of what leadership means and how to be a good leader on the surface level: by communicating well, being honest and listening to others. Whilst all these aspects are crucial in making a good leader, Sharan reminded me of the real reason anyone becomes a leader: to change something they are passionate about. I think this value is important for any leader or follower to uphold in the 21st century.

Throughout Sharan's talk, I couldn't help but think that if every other head of state or head of governmental body had the same empathetic, decency-driven view towards global issues as Sharan did, many more lives would be happier. She reminded us, that it is up to the new generation of leaders to make this positive change happen.

7

The Role of Science and Policy in a Post-Pandemic World

Alan Finkel

27th November 2020

Australia's Chief Scientist's job description is to advise the Prime Minister, the science minster and other ministers; to engage with the public; and to assist the government on international science initiatives. Mostly there's two types of activities: the first is where I'm asked to lead a review and report back to the government with recommendations on a topic, and that uses up perhaps 60% of my time. The second is a combination of engaging with the public through speeches and developing new programs for public benefit. During my nearly five years in the role, I have delivered nearly 100 formal speeches and participated in another 400 less formal presentations such as leading a roundtable discussion or being a discussion panel member.

For the development of new programs, my office staff

and I brainstorm ideas and we jointly implement them. I tend to get all the credit, but I am very dependent on my twelve office staff.

The new programs tend to be self-initiated. For example, we conceived of a program called the Science Policy Fellowship. Here we find a slot in a federal government department for a post-doctoral fellow who is at a career-defining moment, where they don't really know if they want to stay in research, but they have an interest in how their scientific expertise might be used in a policy setting. We ran this as a pilot program and over three years we've placed just over 30 post-docs as one-year full-time employees in various federal government departments. And it has been splendidly successful. Two-thirds of them have chosen to stay on with the federal government department, and the departments love them because they're coming in, not to tell the government how to run science, but to be part of a policy team. These post-doctoral fellows contribute to the team as individuals who have data and analytics capabilities, and project management capabilities, through the lens of their scientific interests and insights.

Also, as a part of the self-initiated quantum, we've developed a website called the STARportal which is like a dating website for extra-curricular science, technology, engineering and mathematics (STEM) activities. Through this portal, providers of extra-curricular activities are visible to students, parents and teachers. Their offerings are the sorts of activities you would do in a science or technology area on nights, weekends or during vacations. For another example, starting with the Australian Government census that is run every five years, the staff in my office spent a couple of years ripping it to pieces and reassembling it through the lens of science and technology to identify career opportunities, salaries, diversity issues, gender issues, etcetera. We also started a program of providing forward-looking visionary advice to government through a program called the Horizon Scanning Reports, where we have looked at things such as synthetic biology, precision medicine, battery storage, agriculture, and the Internet of Things. Each of those are fairly substantial reports. We start by finding a government department that is interested in the topic and they fund it and then we engage the best academics in the country to do the report.

The last self-initiated activity was one of the most important. We started it this year in response to COVID-19 and the recognition of the need to bring evidence-based advice to government. I'm sure that the means of generating advice to government is a question some of you will have. It's called the Rapid Research Information Forum – the RRIF. The purpose is to rapidly provide reports in response to a single question. The questions have to come from an Australian Government minister, and they have to be related to the COVID-19 pandemic. We get them an answer, a written 1500-word response, in 10 to 14 days. It's novel in government. I don't think it's ever been done before, certainly not in the Australian Government. And they love it. There are no recommendations, there are no requests for money. It's just the minister asked a question; it could be, "What is the likely long-term impact of home-schooling on the educational outcomes of Australians?" Or it could be to do with the sensitivities, selectivity and utility of serological antibody tests in managing COVID-19. They've all been initiated on the request from government.

Separately, I've led about a dozen major reviews at the request of the Australian Government. The big one that I did on electricity in 2016 and 2017 became known as the Finkel Review.

If you sit around waiting, and this is my most important message to you, if you sit around waiting, nothing happens. Being active made me visible to government, because even if you are appointed as the Chief Scientist, that doesn't mean anybody ever thinks of you or cares. They're busy. I was doing the electricity review, and that in itself was a coincidence. I happened to be giving a speech at a school called Scotch College. I was the keynote speaker for them launching a new science building. So, it was like 1,000 parents and philanthropists in the audience, including Josh Frydenberg, who you know of as the Treasurer, but back then he was the energy minister. Josh and I knew each other, but not well. He saw me and said, "Oh Alan, I need to speak to you later." Somehow, just the fact that I was there triggered something for him. Eleven o'clock that night I got a phone call from Josh Frydenberg saying, "Oh Alan, I've just been on the phone with the Prime Minister we've been talking about the blackout in South Australia and everybody's upset and there just has to be a review and we think you should be the Chair of the Review." And as I was composing my response which would have been, "B-b b-b b-but that's too hard!" He said, "And I'm so tired." And he hung up on me. And that's how the original Finkel Review began!

The hydrogen review wasn't conceptually initiated by government even though officially it was. What happened is that after the electricity review, at least a dozen or more people from big businesses, and small, said, "Alan, you've been doing all this work on electricity, what about hydrogen?" My response was, "What about hydrogen?" I didn't have an opinion about hydrogen at all. If I had an opinion, it would have been quite cynical and dismissive. But then, because they were all asking, I started looking into it and I realised there was something substantial. I invited about 10 or 12 experts into a discussion group. We had one meeting, and we realised that there was something important here, but then I didn't call a second meeting because I didn't know what to do with it.

What I did instead was that I called Josh Frydenberg, as the energy minister, and said, "Josh, what do you know about hydrogen?" He said, "Nothing substantial." I said, "You need to know about hydrogen!" And he replied, "Well alright, come and tell me." He's a nice guy and so a few weeks later, I visited and gave him a verbal briefing from what I'd picked up from the discussion group and other conversations I had with others. Josh then flagged that he would formally ask me to just bring a briefing document – not a review, a briefing document – to the Council of Australian Governments (COAG) Energy Council. That's the meeting of the energy ministers from all the states and territories in the Commonwealth. With Peta's (Director of the Liveris Academy) help and the help of about another 10 others, at our own cost. No one got paid, there was no funding for this. We didn't do the typical black text on white page, five-page briefing document. We did a 60-page graphical vision statement called 'Hydrogen for Australia's Future'. They were impressed by that, and then on the basis of that vision statement, they asked me to start the development of a hydrogen strategy for the whole of the nation. And at that point it became formal.

Without the initiative, without doing things, nothing would have happened. What I'm saying is if I just sat around saying, "Well, I'm Chief Scientist, people should respect me, and they should come to me for advice." I would have had the most boring five years of my life. But I can tell you I probably had the most intense, exciting and interesting five years of my life and it finishes in 34 days. Not my life, but my role as Chief Scientist finishes at midnight on December the 31st. Now as a result of having done all of that, I've got the ear of the Prime Minister and other ministers and it's a real joy to be able to engage. Ministers come in all shapes and sizes. As somebody at the far end of a television screen you'd probably think they're all pretty drippy. But actually, some of the ministers are super intelligent, they're just constrained by political issues that they have to address in everything they say. But when you're dealing with them in private, it can be extremely pleasant.

I'm sure you have discussions on leadership, and often you'll hear people say, "Leaders are visionary and can communicate that vision," and then that concept will get elaborated on and becomes what people will talk about in terms of leadership. It's only half the story. Really good leaders are also across the operational details and can make things happen. And when you get a leader who tries to float above the operational details, organisations crumble. What I tried to do is, yes, worry about strategy and communicating the strategy, but also get into the operational details because that's what underpins the quality. If you don't look at the details, you won't have a quality high-end product if you haven't underpinned it with quality foundations.

> **If you want cut-through when you have to deliver a piece of scientific advice or a message to people, do you think that people are more likely to respond if it's delivered with optimism or if it relies on the fear factor? – *Scholar, Amber Spurway***

I don't focus on either. I think that I give my best results by delivering advice that is truly based on evidence and careful analysis, but delivered with clarity and enthusiasm. And that enthusiasm is often interpreted as optimism, but sometimes it's not. It could be advice to say, "Don't go this route." But politicians have to make significant decisions. The advice that somebody like me gives them is only one input, and I typically only get one chance to provide that advice. So, I like to go in very well-prepared. I don't put anything in writing or verbally to anybody, and certainly not to ministers and prime ministers unless I'm confident that there's a credible base behind it. Now I don't show off by doing a one-page document with 100 references. I never put references in anything I write for a minister or prime minister, and I try to get it down to one page instead of 10 pages. But every word on that one page needs to be clear in the way that the ideas are articulated and absolutely defensible. If it's evidence-based, it's hard for them to ignore it.

People do talk about getting attention by building up the fear factor or getting people excited by building up the optimism. I think optimism is probably valuable. I am, by my nature, very positive about things, and I think that optimism has a role. But I wouldn't deliberately play it. It's got to emerge from what you know and from what the evidence says.

During the COVID-19 pandemic, why do you think some governments have not listened to scientists and how can that be avoided in the future? – *Scholar, Esandi Kalugalage*

I'd question the premise of what you stated, especially being here in Australia. It is a reality that no governments are perfect. None of them are going to act on scientific advice alone. And you know what, they shouldn't just take science into account. They've got to take community preferences into account. They have to take economics into account. They have to take previous policy commitments they're trying to honour into account. Science is very important, but it's just one piece of information or evidence they have to take into account.

I think Australia has been the world's best practice this year. We've ended up in a fantastic place because of a few unusual factors. One of them is the collegiate government. The Prime Minister Scott Morrison created this new entity called National Cabinet, where I think when they first started it was meeting every week, but now on a less regular basis, perhaps every month. The state premiers and the Prime Minister meet to talk about COVID-19-related and disaster-related issues. And whilst the newspapers might focus on where they disagree, the fact is that the amount of agreement has been extraordinary.

The collegiate government we have seen in Australia this year is the antithesis of what you're seeing in the United States where President Trump is deliberately divisive. Now, I don't know if you have heard Joe Biden give any speeches in the last month or so, including his Thanksgiving speech. If you didn't see his Thanksgiving speech, it's probably worth having a look. He's going overboard to try to be a healing voice and try to bring everybody together for a common purpose. Well, we've seen COVID-19 being regarded by all governments as a medical threat. COVID-19, the virus, is the enemy, not the other state, nor the people, nor industry. Of course, nothing's perfect. And some states go overboard, and some don't do enough. But overall, we've come through this incredibly well. We had a bad spike in Victoria but they've controlled it, because of collegiate government and listening to medical advice and then communicating to the community clearly and consistently. That medical advice has come from Brendan Murphy, the Chief Medical Officer, and his successor Paul Kelly, but it's not them as individuals alone.

There's an entity you wouldn't have heard of called the Australian Health Protection Principals Committee – the AHPPC. Its membership is the chief medical officers from all the states and territories. They meet very frequently, at least weekly. They're informed by expert committees. One is the Public Health Laboratory Network which has all the pathology lab expertise. Another is called the Communicable Diseases Network of Australia (CDNA). They develop the guidelines, including for this year the guidelines for COVID-19. There are a number of other committees, and all of those are synthesised through the AHPPC, and Paul Kelly is invited to every single National Cabinet meeting to explain the public health issues to the Prime Minister and the premiers. He goes out behind the lectern alongside the Prime Minister to speak to the press at the end of every National Cabinet meeting. There's been an extraordinary level of input from the public health sector. Then there are the various medical researchers and institutes. In particular, the Doherty Institute in Melbourne has extraordinary capability on validating diagnostic tests and treatments. Their input is enormously valued in the system. It's quite remarkable to see the system in action.

One other thing I'll mention is to do with the Rapid Research Information Forum (RRIF) that I was talking about before. The very first question we got was at the beginning of April 2020, from the Prime Minister, and Minister for Health Greg Hunt. It was a phone call to me, "Alan, can your group, this RRIF, answer the question, are we likely to see the COVID-19 pandemic get worse in winter?" It was April, in the Southern Hemisphere, which meant we were coming into winter in a few months. It was a fair question. And 10 days later they received a simple answer.

The answer, by the way, is that winter itself doesn't make

it worse, it's the behaviours associated with winter that make it worse, and these can often be managed by communication to people. So, we've got the RRIF as a useful forum that's come out of this year that we didn't have previously. So, the question is, can we capture these lessons learnt and keep the role of public health, medical health, broader scientific issues and also social science issues on the table? Can we continue to have all of that evidence-based advice heard by governments? So, we're trying to make the RRIF permanent even though it was set up for COVID-19. There's a process going on at the moment that by sometime next year, hopefully by the May budget if all goes well, might see it become permanent. And that would be a significant step up in terms of the best academic experts in Australia reporting back up through ministers to government.

So, look, it's far from perfect. But it's a lot better than America. What we don't have, though, is appreciation for the institutions that trained the academics. I don't know what it is, but ministers, backbenchers, parliamentarians in general don't love universities, don't love fundamental research. They think that all research should be commercialisation research. And that's been a hard nut to crack. So whilst I think listening to research is going quite well, that is 'science for policy' is going well, we are not seeing the opposite, which is 'policy for science', doing as well. And I haven't been able to resolve that.

Are Australia's commitments to the Paris Agreement enough, and are they actually still even achievable? – *Scholar, Simeon Gover*

The answer to that is a political answer because if you just went on science you would say that we have to shut down everything that produces carbon dioxide today. Because the reality is, on the collective program of commitments, for Paris, there's no way we are going to restrict temperature rises to one and a half degree Celsius. Highly unlikely we'll keep temperature rises down to two degrees. The world is on track for three degrees. So, the science would therefore say, "Stop now!" Hard stop! But that would destroy civilisation as we know it. Literally, destroy the economy, destroy health, destroy everything.

So the challenge is to move as fast as we can while capitalising on that transition to build the economy. Most people think of it as a dichotomy, either you've got to reduce emissions and stop global warming, or you've got to invest in the economy at the expense of emissions. Realistically, no government anywhere can make a choice like that. If they do make a choice, it will be to preserve the economy and forget about the emissions. So, we need to help governments make a choice to do both. I think the Australian Government is starting to do that.

One thing that the government has done very well was the Renewable Energy Target, the RET, which started in the early 2000s, and got to its end point early this year. That brought the first wave of solar rooftops, solar farms and wind farms into the market. That started as a concept back in 2001 and was really nothing significant, but then found its feet. They tried to do a carbon tax, but it was political suicide. Prime ministers and opposition leaders have just lost their positions by trying to bring in carbon taxes. I'm not talking about the merits of a carbon tax, I'm just saying it's political suicide.

In the 2017 Finkel Review, I tried to get something specific for climate change but the government couldn't go for it, and they brought in the National Energy Guarantee, the NEG, in lieu of that. However, the then Prime Minister, Malcolm Turnbull, lost his job partly because of the NEG. It's really difficult! But what the Finkel Review did do is it recommended two things that have enabled us to bring a lot more solar and wind into the market.

First, we made recommendations that modernised the connection requirements for solar and wind, because as good as solar and wind generators are from the point of view of reducing emissions, they are nasty kids in the neighbourhood when it comes to behaving in electrical grids. It's too complicated to go into now, but instead of adding to the stability of the system, they detract from the stability of the system. So, the rules needed to be modernised so that the system could cope with that.

Second, we made recommendations to change the way that long-distance inter-connectors are committed. That's called the Integrated System Plan. The Australian Energy Market Operator has done two generations of that and now they're designing the long-distance electrical connectors for the national benefit. The intention is to make sure you can bring electrons from where they're generated to where they're needed. And we proposed the creation of Renewable Energy Zones so that governments can allow the funding of inter-connectors into fabulously well-resourced solar and wind zones where no one has built anything yet. Previously, they wouldn't put a transmission line into a renewable energy area because there were no generators to use it. Conversely, no one would build solar and wind in a Renewable Energy Zone because there was no transmission line to take it to the users. We resolved all of those issues, and Australia is now investing per capita in solar and wind at the fastest rate in the world. In 2018, 2019 and again even this year, we've been putting solar and wind in collectively at 10 times the international average per capita. Per capita that's three times more than Germany. You don't hear that out there but it's a fact.

Another big commitment is the Australian National Hydrogen Strategy that we've talked about. It will take years to have an impact, but eventually the impact will be extremely significant at a global level. And our National Hydrogen Strategy is well reputed internationally. We've now got four bilateral partnerships, government to government, based on that. And every state and territory, and private investors, are putting money into developing hydrogen production and utilisation projects. So, it's happening.

The most significant of all was the Low Emissions Technology Statement (LETS), or the Low Emissions Technology Roadmap. I urge you to look it up, the Low Emissions Technology Statement. Look for that phrase with Finkel and you'll find that it's a plan that was put out by the government through the energy minister, Angus Taylor. The government owns the plan. It was put out in September 2020, and it's covering a technology-driven reduction in emissions, into the future, across the economy. In future versions it will consider agriculture, transport, industry, the built environment, and electricity. It's already looking at clean hydrogen, zero emission steel, zero emission aluminium. It is looking at batteries so that solar and wind can be supported as they come onto the market.

People who haven't read the LETS just assume it's about carbon capture and storage for coal-fired electricity. It's not. They assume it's about bringing more gas into the market, it's not. It's batteries so you don't need gas. It's a pivot point. It's actually a direction for the future. Now if you took those three things, the electricity review, the hydrogen strategy and the whole-of-economy LETS and you look at the direction they are taking us, it's a good direction. And if the government had a 2050 commitment now for net zero, these are the initial steps that they would be implementing. Interestingly, the vast majority of people don't see it, but the people in industry are quite excited by the commitments the government is making at the moment.

Is what we're doing enough? It's never enough. And I'm hoping that in the course of the next year that the government will step up their commitments. They have already declared, and this is probably the most important thing of all, they've already declared that they will produce a whole-of-economy low emissions strategy for presentation to the COP26 – the United Nations Climate Change Conference of the Parties – meeting in Glasgow next year. We lost a year because of COVID-19 but it's effectively the five-year update to the Paris meeting, and it's where nations are meant to strengthen their commitments. And in February of this year, the government committed to producing a new strategy to take to the COP26 meeting.

I don't know what's in the strategy. Of course, I've got some behind-the-scenes ideas about it and about where it's going. But it's a big thing. It's difficult for the government. Imagine you're the prime minister of Australia, you've got people who are genuinely concerned and are pushing with their votes to say, "You must do something to reduce emissions more quickly." And then you've got other politicians, particularly ones from a state you might've heard of called Queensland, who say, "The only way forward is to build more coal-fired power stations." And the poor prime minister has to balance all of that. Given that pressure, it's quite remarkable what we've seen come out of the LETS.

Is the benefit of hydrogen worth its major costs and the time to implement, or should we be spending our funds on more solar and wind and other renewable technologies? – *Scholar, Victoria Barnes*

I think the answer is yes, it's absolutely worth it. One of my biggest fears about energy supply going forward is losing diversity of supply. In order for you to calibrate the significance of me even caring about that, consider this. If you got rid of modern medicine, as a civilisation we would be back to the Renaissance period. If you got rid of modern education, we'd be back to the Middle Ages, perhaps. If you got rid of modern energy supplies, we would actually be back to the Stone Age. There's nothing our civilisation depends on more than energy.

If you've got energy, you can pump water; if you can pump water, you can grow food; if you can grow food, you can create a township. Then put your kids into educational environments, start teaching them and develop things and actually have some rules and some civilisation. So, energy is critically important, and our energy needs are going in one direction all the time, and that's up, up, up, and up. You might find that in highly developed countries like Germany, the UK and ultimately Australia, it might go down per capita, but in India and China it's going up, and rapidly, as they're emerging from massive poverty into massive middle-class.

So we need, not a bit, but lots and lots of energy. At the moment we've got seven significant energy sources. Globally, we have coal, oil, natural gas, nuclear, large-scale hydroelectricity, solar and wind. There's nothing else of significance. Sources such as wave power, tidal power, even bio-fuels, don't have the potential to reach the scale of those seven. But we are saying to ourselves, we don't want to use coal. Which is fine. We don't want to use oil and we don't want to use natural gas. So now we're down to four. In most countries, we're saying we don't want to use nuclear, so now we're down to three. In most modern countries, we're saying we don't want to flood valleys and have new hydroelectricity, so we're down to two. Which is solar and wind. Okay, I know that the sun is not going to run out, I know there will always be wind, but it's scary, nevertheless. Because unimaginable things like a volcanic eruption that literally disturbs climate for six weeks can happen and has happened in the past. Clouds and no wind, not a good combination. And then there are the resources required. Because we're not talking about a little bit of solar and a little bit of wind to replace all the oil, coal and gas and nuclear that we use today. We have to increase our solar and wind investment to 40 or 50 times more than all the solar and wind that we have today.

So, we need supply diversity. For diversity, I'm going a step further to say not only invest in hydrogen but also think about investing in hydrogen from fossil fuels. Because you can make hydrogen from coal gasification or a natural gas process with carbon capture and storage. And then you've got hydrogen as a burnable fuel and a chemical feedstock that doesn't require all that solar and wind to make it. But if you put that to the side, and imagine a world that is fundamentally getting all of its energy from solar and wind – electrons are marvellous and you can use them for a huge range of things – it is still a challenge to work out how to run an electric planet in which all the electricity is used as electrons.

Sometimes you need a high-density transportable fuel. Sometimes you want to do what Australia wants to do, which is export renewable energy from one continent to another continent. Well, good luck doing that with undersea cables. I can't conceive of anything more strategically risky or expensive. But if you can convert that electricity into hydrogen or ammonia, either way, you can now ship it. If you can convert the renewable electricity into hydrogen, you can make ammonia to make fertiliser, and now you can have zero emissions fertiliser. Well, electrons can't do that for you. If you convert electricity into hydrogen, you can now make zero emission steel, and that's really significant. Note that steel making, I'm not talking about industry as a whole, but just steel making, is responsible for 7% of global carbon dioxide emissions. It is massive.

The only way you can replace all the coal, the metallurgical coal, a special kind of high-purity coal that is used to make steel and is responsible for 7% of emissions, is to replace the heating role of the coal with renewable electricity. And replace the chemical role which I won't go into now but it's a big role, the chemical role of the carbon in the coal with hydrogen. So, with hydrogen made from renewable electricity we can get rid of a source of 7% of emissions, literally like that. It costs a lot of money now and may take a few years to scale up, but literally, we would be making zero emission steel to replace what we've got at the moment. So I'm not suggesting that hydrogen is an alternative to solar and wind, but I am saying that the modelling that has been done, leaving aside that whatever a model predicts you know will be wrong, predicts that probably 15%, maybe up to 20%, of end use of energy will be hydrogen molecules instead of electrons.

Scholar Reflection – Flynn Pearman

When it comes to government decision-making, we as the public seldom realise the true processes behind these decisions. Perhaps during the COVID-19 pandemic it has become a bit more evident. Speaking with Dr Alan Finkel, the former Chief Scientist of Australia, was a revelation in terms of understanding the inner workings of government policy decision-making – particularly relating to the role of science. The announcements we see in the media really are just the tip of the iceberg.

This interaction between the various scientific fields, their experts, and the policymakers is critical in ensuring evidence-based decision-making is a cornerstone of the Australian Government. In his role as Chief Scientist, it was encouraging to hear how Dr Finkel was committed to making scientific knowledge easily accessible to ministers and their offices, through initiatives such as the Rapid Research Information Forum (RRIF) and countless reviews. He put great emphasis on the concise delivery of information to these leaders. He said he used one page instead of 10 to summarise robust, defensible recommendations. This was a great reminder for anyone trying to communicate effectively. With the COVID-19 pandemic, we have seen the value in considered, evidence-based decision-making in politics and engaging experts in direct communication with the public. I believe this approach to consolidating and publicly disseminating information is a fine way to address the array of global challenges in the 21st century.

Dr Finkel's journey to Chief Scientist was winding, yet extremely interesting and unique. As a young man still finding his path, it resonated to hear his rationale behind many of his career decisions: do things that are engaging to you and jump on opportunities. By making the most of his opportunities, Dr Finkel's journey is affirmation of how this philosophy removes any ceiling on the impact and diversity of one's career. Nonetheless, for me perhaps his most poignant message was, "if you sit around waiting it doesn't happen." I feel like this adage is especially true in government and whilst apparently obvious, a great reminder for emerging leaders in the 21st century.

8

Conclusions: A Conversation is the Smallest Unit of Change

Tim Kastelle

A big part of leadership is dealing with change. As James Carse said, "Only that which can change can continue".[5] In this set of conversations with leaders, change is evident throughout. The Dow Chemical that Andrew Liveris recently left is far different from the Dow Chemical that he joined over 40 years earlier. As evident from his conversation here, he is a different Andrew Liveris as well. We can see similar amounts of change in all of the leaders highlighted in this book, as well as in the organisations and people with which they have been involved.

I focus on change because it highlights the key elements of leadership. My area of specialisation is innovation – how people and organisations can use new ideas to create value. In other words, how ideas create change. Even with the

5 James Carse, *Finite and Infinite Games* (New York: Simon & Schuster, 2013).

internet and all of the other new technologies and forms of communication available to us today, ideas create change only as they pass from one person to another. Most of the time, this happens through conversations – which makes this book particularly relevant today, as it reports on a series of dialogues between global leaders and university students.

Two things really stuck with me while participating in these discussions as they happened. The first was the quality and depth of the questions that the scholars asked. They seemed to be able to hone in on the critical experiences in the careers of each of the leaders, and asked the right questions to bring out responses to one of the unspoken questions throughout these conversations: "What can the lessons you've learnt through your experience help me prepare for mine?" The second thing that struck me was the openness and eagerness the leaders showed in engaging with these questions. Despite differences in age and experiences, there was a high level of mutual respect shown throughout the conversations.

Writing these reflections only weeks after the most recent report from the Intergovernmental Panel on Climate Change was released, while still in the middle of a global pandemic, brings home the importance of all of us learning these lessons. How can we have an impact on these challenges ourselves? There are lessons throughout these conversations.

The critical importance of discussion and engagement is evident throughout all six conversations. One of the most striking examples comes from Ginni Rometty, discussing IBM's response to the killing of George Floyd. After talking with thousands of IBM's Black employees, the issues that they still experience based simply on the colour of their skin were shocking. Rometty said:

> I think when you see that so closely, I don't know how you can't permanently be changed. All the issues and solutions start at home. So, even in the company that I thought I was doing such a great job, I thought I can do a lot better. So we're going to do a lot better.

And the consequence was a series of substantial changes in the way the company operates. That's change coming directly through conversation – conversation, and often compromise.

Which leads to a second important lesson: in a complex environment, our dilemmas seldom have clear-cut solutions that are guaranteed to work. There's always uncertainty. In my own field, if we know in advance that a new idea will work, by definition it's not innovative. Change requires uncertainty. Which, in turn, means that most of the problems that are framed as either/or dichotomies actually need to be addressed as issues that require a both/and response.

This shows up most clearly in Paul Polman's example of generating change in the clothing industry through developing industry-wide collaboration. This was necessary to get away from the zero-sum win/lose dichotomy:

> The crucial factor is getting stakeholders in the industry together. The entire way we've set up our private sector is around a win/lose dichotomy – if I do something, it has to

> be to my advantage, and it has to be to your disadvantage. It's a secret what I do and I should keep it to myself. However, what we're saying here is the price for humanity is much higher than for your individual gain. It's a bit of the prisoner's dilemma. If we all don't do it together, we all go under. And this is really what we're talking about now, especially when it gets to planetary boundaries.

In this case, the outcome is a change in the way an industry operates. The innovation here is about the way in which industry players adopt new ideas and new technologies, not the new technologies themselves. This is almost always the case. New ideas and new technologies can trigger change, but only when they cause people to change their behaviour. And behaviour change happens when we talk to each other.

Of course, conversation can be used to drive change that isn't widely beneficial. When this is done at scale, it's propaganda. And conversation can be used at an interpersonal level to manipulate and mislead as easily as it can be used to inspire. The type of change we want to participate in is critically important. This leads to the final lesson that I take from these discussions: purpose is essential.

Again, this theme came up through all of the discussions. Ajay Banga makes the point mostly clearly in discussing his time at Mastercard:

> I think the one thing I feel very good about in my voice is that I've made meaning out of standard phrases like 'you can do well by doing good'. I have proven in our company that you can do that. And I have led on financial inclusion around

> the world, making it a part of our business model. You can do well by doing good. I started out with a $20 billion market cap company that's now $300+ billion, depending on the day you look at the share price. I think if you can do that while attempting to get 500 million people out of financial exclusion into it that is an achievement and shows you can lead with doing good.

The drive to reduce financial exclusion came first – the purpose. This then led to strategies designed to address this issue. Executing them successfully drove the substantial increase in the firm's market capitalisation. Every leader here speaks about a purpose that they're passionate about, and which drove their strategy just as financial inclusion drove Banga's.

There is a similar process at work in the course of individual change. Conversations can lead to a change in mindset. When this change is salient enough to one's identity and purpose, the new mindset will lead to change in behaviour.

We can see these mindset shifts happening in the scholars' reflections on the sessions. In nearly every case, the reflection talks about a change in belief triggered by the discussion. Here is Lilly Van Gilst's reflection on Polman's talk:

> In the past, I have perceived a dichotomy between being profitable in business and doing what is right by people and the environment. However, Paul's ideas and methods provide a crucial reframing, showing that not only is doing good

> things possible as a business leader, it is the fundamental tenet upon which to act.

If you revisit the scholars' reflections, you'll see something like this in every one of them. And so, we see conversations triggering change at multiple levels – within individuals, companies, and entire industries. The problems that we face today often can seem overwhelming. But the conversations recorded in this book show us many examples of leading change. And in nearly every case, that change starts with a conversation.

About the Leaders

Andrew N. Liveris AO

Founding Donor of the Andrew N. Liveris Academy for Innovation and Leadership, and former Chairman and CEO of the Dow Chemical Company.

Andrew N. Liveris is the former chairman and chief executive officer of the Dow Chemical Company and the former executive chairman of DowDuPont. With over forty years of global leadership experience at the Dow Chemical Company, his career has included roles in manufacturing, engineering, sales, marketing, and business and general management around the world.

Andrew serves as a trustee for the King Abdullah University of Science and Technology (KAUST), the Minderoo Foundation, and the United States Council for International Business, and was recently appointed chairman of the Australian Government's National COVID-19 Coordination Commission's Manufacturing Taskforce.

Previously, he was the vice-chair of the Business Roundtable, an executive committee member and chairman of the United States Business Council, and a member of the Concordia Leadership Council and the Australian Government's Industry Growth Centres Advisory Committee.

He earned a bachelor's degree (first-class honours) in

chemical engineering from the University of Queensland and was awarded the University Medal for that year. In 2005, he was awarded an honorary doctorate in science by his alma mater as well as being named Alumnus of the Year.

Andrew was appointed Officer of the Order of Australia for his services to international business in 2014.

Ajay Banga

Executive Chairman, and former CEO and President of Mastercard.

Ajay Banga is the executive chairman of the board of directors and the former chief executive officer of Mastercard. Prior to Mastercard, Ajay served as chief executive officer of Citigroup Asia Pacific. He also oversaw the company's efforts in microfinance. He is a graduate of Delhi University and the Indian Institute of Management, Ahmedabad.

Ajay is a co-founder of the Cyber Readiness Institute, chairman of the International Chamber of Commerce and a trustee of the United States Council for International Business. Ajay is a founding trustee of the US-India Strategic Partnership Forum, a member of the US-India CEO Forum and is chairman emeritus of the American India Foundation. He served as a member of President Obama's Commission on Enhancing National Cybersecurity. He is a past member of the US President's Advisory Committee for Trade Policy and Negotiations.

He was awarded the Padma Shri Award by the President of India in 2016, the Ellis Island Medal of Honor in 2019 and the Business Council for International Understanding's Global Leadership Award. He is a fellow of the Foreign Policy Association and was awarded the Foreign Policy Association Medal in 2012.

Paul Polman

Co-Founder and Chair of IMAGINE, and former CEO of Unilever

Paul Polman is co-founder and chair of IMAGINE, a benefit corporation and foundation accelerating business leadership to achieve the global goals. He is also chair of the International Chamber of Commerce, the B Team, Saïd Business School and the Valuable 500, and vice-chair of the UN Global Compact. He was CEO of Unilever for a decade.

Paul was appointed to the UN Secretary General's High-Level Panel that developed the Sustainable Development Goals (SDG) and was a founder member of the Business & Sustainable Development Commission.

He founded the Kilimanjaro Blind Trust with Kim Polman, working to improve the lives of blind and visually impaired children in East Africa. He is also a counsellor and chair of the Global Advisory Board of One Young World.

He has received numerous awards, including the Rainforest Alliance Lifetime Achievement Award, the UN Environment Programme's Champion of the Earth Award and the Oslo Business for Peace Award.

He received France's Chevalier de la Légion d'Honneur, and was named an Honorary Knight Commander of the Order of the British Empire for services to business. He is a recipient of the Public Service Star from the Government of Singapore and received the Treaty of Nijmegen Medal.

Ginni Rometty

Executive Chairman, and former Chairman, President and CEO of IBM

Virginia (Ginni) Rometty is executive chairman of IBM and was IBM's chairman, president and chief executive officer. Under Ginni's leadership, IBM expanded capabilities in hybrid cloud, security, quantum computing, industry expertise, and data and AI. Ginni also established IBM as the model of responsible stewardship in the digital age, advocating for technology ethics and data stewardship.

Under her leadership, IBM created thousands of 'new collar' jobs and championed the reinvention of education around the world, including the explosive growth of the six-year Pathways in Technology Early College High Schools (P-TECHs), which are serving hundreds of thousands of students in 24 countries for disadvantaged populations.

IBM also achieved record results in diversity and inclusion under Ginni's leadership. This pioneering work was recognised in 2018 by the prestigious Catalyst Award for advancing diversity and women's initiatives.

Ginni has a Bachelor of Science degree with high honours in computer science and electrical engineering from Northwestern University.

She serves on the Council on Foreign Relations, the board of trustees of Northwestern University, the boards of overseers and managers of Memorial Sloan-Kettering Cancer Center, and the board of directors of JPMorgan Chase & Co. She is co-chair of the Aspen Institute's Cyber Group, a member of the advisory board of Tsinghua University School of Economics and Management, and a member of the Singapore Economic Development Board International Advisory Council.

Sharan Burrow AC

Secretary-General, International Trade Union Confederation, Brussels

Sharan Burrow is the general secretary of the International Trade Union Confederation (ITUC), representing 200 million workers in 163 countries and territories with 332 national affiliates.

Prior to this, she held the position of ITUC president since its Founding Congress in Vienna and the position of International Confederation of Free Trade Unions (ICFTU) president since its 18th World Congress in Miyazaki (November 2004). She is the first woman to have held any of these positions. She was president of the Australian Council of Trade Unions (ACTU).

Sharan is a passionate advocate and campaigner for social justice, women's rights, the environment and labour law reforms, and has led union negotiations on major economic reforms and labour rights campaigns in her home country of Australia and globally.

In October 2000, Sharan also became the first woman to be elected president of the International Confederation of Free Trade Unions Asia Pacific Region Organisation.

She has also served as a member of the Governing Body of the International Labour Organisation (ILO) and a member of the Stakeholder Council of the Global Reporting Initiative. As part of her ILO responsibilities, Sharan chaired the Workers' Group of the Sub-Committee on Multinational Enterprises.

Sharan has received a Companion of the Order of Australia Award for achievement and merit of the highest degree in service to Australia or to humanity at large.

Alan Finkel AO

Australia's former Chief Scientist

Dr Alan Finkel was Australia's Chief Scientist. Prior to his appointment, he served as president of the Australian Academy of Technology and Engineering (ATSE), and for eight years as chancellor of Monash University. At ATSE, he led the development and implementation of the STELR program which has been adopted in more than 600 Australian schools.

As Chief Scientist, Alan was appointed chair of the Expert Advisory Panel for the CSIRO Report on Climate and Disaster Resilience, and chair of the Technology Investment Roadmap Ministerial Reference Group. He led the development of the 2019 National Hydrogen Strategy, the National Research Infrastructure Roadmap, the Review into the National Electricity Market ('Finkel Review'), and the STEM Industry Partnership Forum report. He serves as the Deputy Chair of Innovation and Science Australia.

Alan has an extensive science background as an entrepreneur, engineer, neuroscientist and educator. He co-founded Cosmos Magazine, which in addition to magazine publishing operates a secondary schools science education program.

He was awarded his PhD in electrical engineering from Monash University and worked as a postdoctoral research fellow in neuroscience at the Australian National University.

Alan was the 2016 Victorian of the Year, received the 2015 IET Mountbatten Medal (UK) and the 2019 IEEE Joseph F. Keithley Award and is a winner of the Clunies Ross Award.